FACING LIFE'S PROBLEMS

Also available in the "How to" series:

Battle for the Mind	David Holden
Effective Evangelism	Ben Davies
Enjoying God's Grace	Terry Virgo
Growing Up as a Christian	Roger Day
Handling Your Money	John Houghton
Honouring Marriage	John and Liz Wilthew
Joining the Church	Richard Haydon-Knowell
Knowing God's Will	Phil Rogers
Leading a Housegroup	Richard Haydon-Knowell
Learning to Worship	Phil Rogers
Praying the Lord's Prayer	Terry Virgo
Presenting Jesus in the Open Air	Mike Sprenger
Receiving the Holy Spirit and His Gifts	Terry Virgo and Phil Rogers
Seeking the Kingdom	John Hosier

For further information on the "How to" series and other publications, please write to Frontier Publications International, 9 Boundary Road, Hove, BN3 4EH.

SERIES EDITOR
TERRY VIRGO

FACING LIFE'S PROBLEMS

FRANK GAMBLE

FRONTIER PUBLISHING INTERNATIONAL

WORD PUBLISHING
Word (UK) Ltd
Milton Keynes, England
WORD AUSTRALIA
Kilsyth, Victoria, Australia
WORD COMMUNICATIONS LTD
Vancouver, B.C., Canada
STRUIK CHRISTIAN BOOKS (PTY) LTD
Maitland, South Africa
ALBY COMMERCIAL ENTERPRISES PTE LTD
Balmoral Road, Singapore
CHRISTIAN MARKETING NEW ZEALAND LTD
Havelock North, New Zealand
JENSCO LTD
Hong Kong
SALVATION BOOK CENTRE
Malaysia

FACING LIFE'S PROBLEMS
© Frank Gamble 1991.
Published by Word (UK) Ltd/Frontier Publishing International.

ISBN 0-85009-191-8   (Australia 1-86258-176-2)

Unless otherwise indicated, Scripture quotations are from the New
International Version (NIV). Copyright © 1973, 1978, 1984 by
International Bible Society.

Reproduced, printed and bound in Great Britain for Word (UK) Ltd. by
Richard Clay Ltd., Bungay.

91 92 93 94 / 10 9 8 7 6 5 4 3 2 1

FOREWORD

The "How to" series has been published with a definite purpose in view. It provides a set of workbooks suitable either for housegroups or individuals who want to study a particular Bible theme in a practical way. The goal is not simply to look up verses and fill in blank spaces on the page, but to fill in gaps in our lives and so increase our fruitfulness and our knowledge of God.

Both of Peter's letters were written to "stimulate ... wholesome thinking" (2 Peter 3:1). He required his readers to think as well as read! We hope the training manual approach of this book will have the same effect. *Stop*, *think*, *apply* and *act* are key words.

If you are using the book on your own, we suggest you work through the chapters systematically, Bible at your side and pen in hand. If you are doing it as a group activity, it is probably best to do all the initial reading and task work before the group sessions — this gives more time for discussion on key issues which may be raised.

Unless otherwise stated, all quotations from the Bible are from the New International Version which you are, in the main, encouraged to use when you fill in the study material.

Terry Virgo
Series Editor

Special Thanks

I should like to thank Chris Wisdom for his encouragement and advice in the planning of this book, Iona Giagnoni for her help in typing up my notes and Mary Austin for shaping the material.

Frontier Publishing International is committed to the production of printed and recorded materials with the view to reaching this generation with the gospel of the kingdom. FPI is part of New Frontiers International, a team ministry led by Terry Virgo, which is involved in planting and equipping churches according to New Testament principles. New Frontiers International is also responsible for a wide range of training programmes and conferences.

Contents

Introduction

Facing Life's Problems is never easy. Sometimes we encounter one problem after another, and just when it seems that things can't get any worse, they do! Prayers appear to go unanswered and life is one big struggle. We can end up confused and angry. Why does God allow problems and difficulties in our lives? Doesn't He care about us? Is there a reason for suffering and pain?

There are many serious questions which deserve more than just superficial answers. I believe that there are important truths in the Bible which can help us to understand the problems of this life. We can have a new perspective on our troubles and trials which will enable us not only to cope better, but actually to rejoice in them.

As we discover the truth about our problems, we will discover the truth about God. We shall see more clearly His purpose for us and our destiny as His children. We will also establish the fact that God does love and care for us. This truth will steady our hearts and bring new strength and confidence into our lives. Our problems may still be there, but we will see them in a new light and be able to face them with faith and joy.

May the Lord bless you and keep you, and may His grace make you strong and fruitful for his glory.

Frank Gamble

Chapter 1   DON'T BE SURPRISED

I was twenty-six years old; Glenda and I had been married for four years and we had two young children. I was sitting in our local hospital waiting for the results of some X-rays — part of my spine was stiff and I'd been experiencing pain in my lower back. When the specialist called me into her office she had bad news for me. "You've got an incurable and progressive disease" she said. "It will attack every joint in your body, calcify your vertebrae and bend you over like an old man." I heard what she said but the word "incurable" preoccupied my mind.

I had been a Christian for fifteen years and, at the age of nineteen, had gone to Bible College. Now I was pastor of a church in South Harrow — facing a chronic disease. The news naturally shocked me but I didn't panic and go to pieces. My immediate reaction was, "I will put my trust in God. He's my rock and when stormy waves batter me, He's testing the foundations on which my life is built." God had healed me twice before — of baldness and a burst ear drum. He had also healed my mother-in-law of terminal cancer — which significantly raised my level of faith for my own healing. Not for one second did I question the goodness and love of God.

It was 1977 when the specialist first gave me the devastating news. I am now in a wheelchair. Not only do I suffer from severe pain, I also experience acute frustration because I can no longer do the things that I used to take for granted. I can't brush my hair, dress myself, walk or drive. But I'm still trusting God, laying hold of my destiny as His child and living for His glory. He's using this illness for my good. Glenda joyfully affirms that I've changed for the better and our marriage has improved. We now have three wonderful children and

I'm still leading a church! I often think of myself as "The prisoner of the Lord" and I'm confident that He will fulfil His purpose for me.

A. Don't Abandon Truth
In times of crisis or difficulty we must never abandon truth. When I was a civil engineer we used to use an immovable object as a reference point for our instruments. These "reference points" enabled us to tell where we were with regard to the overall plan. Truth is our reference point. The Word is unchanging and endures forever. And it tells us that God is good and God is love.

How do you react to problems? What is your life founded on? If you've heard God's Word but have not obeyed it then you are building your life on sand and the storms of life will shake you badly. If, on the other hand, you have heard the Word of God and obeyed it, then you are unshakeable. You are building your life on a rock which will not crumble or give way (Read Matthew 7:24-27).

Write down some of the difficulties that you have experienced.

1. ....

2. ....

3. ....

4. ....

5. ....

How did you apply God's Word to each situation?

1. ....

2. ....

3. ....

4. ....

5. ....

James tells us, "Do not merely listen to the word, and so deceive yourselves. Do what it says" (Jas 1:22). Clearly, God is looking not just for those who seem keen to hear Him, He is far more concerned that we consistently act on what He says. He is our Creator and He knows what is best for us. If we doubt His word, we are actually doubting His character.

B. The Character of God

If we're going to trust God in difficulties, we must know that He is trustworthy. Is He really loving? Are His motives pure? Does He act haphazardly — suddenly deciding to bless one and crush another just for the sake of it?

Tick the statements about God that you feel are correct:
- ❑ Whenever I suffer, God is punishing me.
- ❑ He doesn't care much about what happens to me.
- ❑ Whatever He does is for my good.
- ❑ He enjoys seeing me suffer.
- ❑ He loves me as His precious child.
- ❑ He always knows exactly what He's doing in my life.
- ❑ His actions are often totally unfair.
- ❑ He is faithful and just in all He does.
- ❑ He is loving in all He does.
- ❑ He's cruel.
- ❑ He rarely listens to me.
- ❑ He wants me to learn something from my trials.

God wants you to be secure when the storm comes. You must know what He is like or you will for ever be shifting on the sands of doubt over what is happening to you.

Here are some things about God that you need to know:

1. God is righteous

The psalmist declares: "Righteous are you, O Lord, and your laws are right" (Psalm 119:137; see also Psalm 145:17). The apostle John uses light as a symbol of righteousness and says, "God is light; in Him there is no darkness at all" (1 John 1:5). Clearly God's righteousness was reflected in His Son's earthly ministry. Jesus said, "I always do what pleases Him" (John 8:29). Everything He did was right — Pilate could find no fault in Him. We can never accuse God of acting wrongly. His ways are perfect.

2. God is just

In righteousness God sets the standard; in justice He upholds it. Abraham questioned, "Will not the Judge of all the earth do right?" (Gen 18:25). Here, God destroyed the guilty but rescued the innocent. When He does not seem to treat people as they deserve, we dare not doubt His justice. God is perfect in His knowledge of every situation and He promises to reward us according to what we have done.

3. God is holy

God is morally perfect. He says, "I am the Lord, your Holy One" (Is 43:15). Since He is always consistent with His character, His holiness will govern the way He acts. Holiness is God's standard for us. Peter says, "Just as He who called you is holy, so be holy in all you do" (1 Pet 1:15). Sin offends God. His wrath against it is not selfish revenge but the revulsion of His holy nature against moral evil.

4. God is true

God is true over against what is false. When Jeremiah was dealing with the people's idolatry he referred to God as "The true God" (Jer 10:10). Jesus said, "I am ... the truth" (John 14:6). When He prayed for His disciples, He asked His Father to "Sanctify them by the truth; your word is truth" (John 17:17). The Bible is totally reliable because God's words are always true.

5. God is faithful

Moses exhorted the Israelites, "Know therefore that the Lord your God is God; He is the faithful God, keeping His covenant of love to a thousand generations of those who love Him and keep His commands" (Deut 7:9). People may let us down but God is always faithful to His promises. If He says something in His Word, we can believe it.

6. God is love

God is love (1 John 4:8), and He loves us with an everlasting love which will never fail (Jer 31:3). The proof of God's love lies in the sacrifice of Jesus for us (Rom 5:8). There is no greater expression of love than that (John 15:13).

Read Moses' comments about God in Deuteronomy 32:4 and write out the verse in sections. Then circle the most significant words and meditate on the verse as a whole.

He is ....

his ....,

and ....

A ....

who ....

....

The Scriptures give us many examples of people who faced suffering and pain. Stephen was stoned, yet he was radiant and able to pray for his murderers. Paul was in jail, yet he could say that God was using his imprisonment to advance the gospel. Jacob was crippled but he leant on his staff and worshipped God. I've heard of many Christians who have gone through all sorts of hardships — even persecution and torture for their faith. They trusted God and He upheld them. I'm no-one special but I've trusted Him and He's upheld me too.

If God allows you to suffer, He will give you the grace to cope. You may be ill, persecuted at work, financially hard up, undergoing spiritual attack or going through a time of severe temptation. Whatever you're facing, you can choose to respond with faith. Know that everything God does is consistent with His perfect character, and that He uses each situation for His purposes and for your good. He wants you to trust His word and His unfailing love.

It is during the dark times that your light can shine the brightest. Your response to your trial will cause others to recognise the reality of your faith. By trusting and obeying Jesus in every situation you will highlight the grace of God in your life to those around you. The constancy of your devotion to Jesus will confirm to you, and to others, the genuineness of your love for the One who gave Himself for you.

Read Philippians 4:13.

What can you do? ....

What will Christ do?...

Read Ephesians 3:20.

What is God able to do?..

....

According to what?...

....

Read Psalm 138:8.

What will God do for you?..

C. Face the Facts
Many Christians are thrown when they encounter problems and difficulties. The main reason for this is the false assumption that God's people should not experience too much suffering or hardship.

The prevailing Christian attitude seems to be that the life of the believer ought, for the large part, to be problem free — like a "top of the range" luxury car that never breaks down, or a dream holiday where the sun never stops shining!

But the Word of God clearly teaches that we should actually expect problems. Jesus said to His disciples, "I have told you these things, so that in me you may have peace. In this world you will have trouble. But take heart! I have overcome the world" (John 16:33). The apostle Paul told the believers at Philippi, "For it has been granted to you on behalf of Christ not only to believe on Him, but also to suffer for Him" (Phil 1:29). Paul knew what he was talking about, because just after his conversion, the Lord spoke to him through Ananias about the suffering he would experience as a Christian (see Acts 9:15,16).

Read 1 Peter 4:12 and 1 John 3:13.
What phrase is repeated in both of these verses?

....

It is not strange then for Christians to experience suffering, and we should not be thrown by problems and painful times. Peter exhorts us not to be ashamed of suffering as Christians but rather to rejoice (1 Pet 4:13,16). We must act on these things if we are going to live for the glory of God.

D. The Mystery of Suffering
One of the mysteries of kingdom life is this: what happens to one person may not happen to another. Christians must come to terms with apparent inconsistencies where suffering is concerned.

James was killed with a sword while Peter was let out of prison by an angel (Acts 12). The apostle Paul was bitten by a snake, healed and given a thorn in the flesh (2 Cor 12:7). Lazarus was raised from the dead (John 11:44).

Hebrews 11 also highlights some of these mysteries. Read Hebrews 11:32-38 and write down some of the contrasting things that happened to these men and women of faith.

....

....

....

....

Where treats are concerned, Glenda and I have never given our children the same. As parents we felt that if one child had something, the others needn't always have the same. Our children have learned that they can't have everything they want, and that they can't have the same as everyone else.

God wants His children to come to terms with the different things that happen to them. This does not mean that we succumb to fatalism. On the contrary, we must be full of faith. But at the same time we must face reality. One person will be healed, another will not. One will recover from serious illness, another will die. Some will experience amazing provision, others will be very hard up. Some will get married, others will stay single. Some will have many children, others only one, and some will not be able to have any children at all.

On the surface it seems that God is very unfair and inconsistent; but He is neither. Our heavenly Father always knows what is best for us and He is also aware of our limitations. At the end of the day, we must acknowledge that He is Sovereign. He made us; He redeemed us; we belong to Him. He is the potter, we are the clay. We have been called according to His purpose. It is not what we want that matters; it is what He wants. Our Lord Jesus always did the Father's will. He suffered physically, emotionally and spiritually, but He still prayed to His Father, "Not my will, but yours be done" (Luke 22:42).

E. The Sufferings of Jesus

Jesus is our example and we are called to live the way He did. Since He was fully human He understands all the problems and sufferings that we go through.

Write down some of the sufferings that Jesus faced during His earthly ministry (eg hunger, disappointment):

....

....

....

....

The focal point of our Lord's suffering is, without question, the cross. Jesus was not afraid of death, but He dreaded the experience of the cross. There was the physical suffering, yes, but the cross meant more than that. Jesus knew that when He took our sin upon Himself, His Father would turn away from Him, pour out His wrath on Him and, for the first time ever, abandon Him. No wonder His "sweat was like drops of blood" (Luke 22:44). No wonder He prayed, "Father, if you are willing, take this cup from me" (Luke 22:42).

The early church found the key to understanding Jesus' suffering in Isaiah 53 (See Acts 8:30ff and 1 Peter 2:22-25).

Read Isaiah 53 and write down some of the things that Jesus suffered:

....

....

....

No matter what it cost Him — physical needs, family pressures or even crucifixion — Jesus fixed His mind and energy on doing the will of God. Many of us do God's will until problems come our way. Then we get side-tracked and slip into anger and self-pity. Jesus is our example. We must follow Him.

When the discs in my spine were disintegrating and my vertebrae were grinding painfully against one another, I thought of Jesus and the agony that He suffered for me.

What I felt was terrible, but it was nothing compared to what He went through. As you face suffering or problems of different kinds, remember that Jesus understands and that through Him you can find grace to help in times of need.

F. The Cost of Discipleship
The Lord Jesus was always very frank about the cost of discipleship. He said to His disciples, "If anyone would come after me, he must deny himself and take up his cross daily and follow me... Any of you who does not give up everything he has cannot be my disciple" (Luke 9:23; 14:33). Discipleship is not easy.

Read 1 Peter 2:20,21.

What have you been called to do?...

Whom are you following?..

Jesus warned His disciples that they would be persecuted, imprisoned and even killed for His sake (Luke 21:12-19).

What are we when we're persecuted?

.... (Matt 5:10,11)

What must we do for our persecutors?

....(Matt 5:44; Rom 12:14).

20

What will be the result of our persecution?

....

(Luke 21:13)

Being a disciple of Jesus involves self-denial, self-discipline and persecution. Have you faced up to the cost of following Jesus? Are you surprised when you face trials of many kinds? You need to readjust your thinking and come to terms with the inevitable difficulties that you will encounter as a Christian.

One of the questions I have been asked more than any other is this: "If God is all-powerful and all-loving, why does He let people suffer?" The question is actually made up of two questions: Why does God allow suffering? How can suffering be reconciled with the love of God? Before we can come up with any answers, we must examine the origin of suffering.

Suffering — Where's It From?

The origin of suffering is directly linked to the origin of evil. When evil came into the world, suffering came with it. The Bible does not say much about the origin of evil, but it apparently reared its head when there was a rebellion in heaven (see Isaiah 14:12-15). The angel, Satan, was once exalted in rank and power above the rest. Then he became proud, sought to elevate himself above God and was cast out of heaven. Several other angels fell with him (Jude 6; 2 Peter 2:4).

Just as Satan was accountable for his actions, so too are we. God has not surrounded Himself with robots who are programmed to obey Him. From the beginning, He decided to give us the option of whether or not to do as He says. This is amazing. He knew the pain that such freedom would bring and how much it would cost Him to redeem us, but He still gave us the opportunity to choose.

This freedom to decide things for ourselves inevitably means that we are responsible for our actions, words and thoughts. Privilege always goes hand in hand with responsibility (see Amos 3:2). When Adam sinned, he tried to blame Eve for his disobedience but God held him accountable for what he had done (Gen 3:12-19). When we sin, there is no point in our trying to blame others. We are guilty and one day we will all stand before God and give account for the things that we have done.

So although we cannot categorically state how and why evil came into being, we can say with certainty that God did not originate it. The Scriptures make it quite clear that Satan is ultimately responsible for all evil and is therefore behind all suffering in the world.

Read 1 John 5:19.
What does this verse tell us about Satan?

....

We can see the results of Satan's rule. He blinds the eyes of unbelievers so that they cannot see or understand the truth. He is the enemy of all righteousness and attacks those who are wanting to live for the glory of God. It is very clear in Scripture that Satan inflicts suffering upon men and women.

A. Satan and Suffering
On one occasion Jesus met a woman who was bent double by her illness.
Read Luke 13:11,16.
Who was responsible for her condition?
❏ herself
❏ God
❏ Satan
❏ someone else
Once Jesus had identified the problem, He laid His hands on her and she was immediately set free.

In the Old Testament, we read about Job's terrible sufferings. When Satan left God's presence the second time, what did he do?

....(Job 2:7)

It is clear from this passage that Satan can do only as much as God allows. Notice that the devil is not omnipresent — he goes to and fro on the earth. And notice too that there are sometimes things happening in the heavenlies of which we are totally unaware. Job didn't know what was going on in heavenly places, but God gives us a glimpse into the background of his story. Without this information we would not understand as fully exactly what was happening to him.

Another individual who suffered at Satan's hands was the apostle Paul.
What did he call his "thorn in the flesh"?

....(2 Cor 12:7)

Satan evidently gave Paul a rough time. The apostle was buffeted and weakened by the attacks, the intensity of which drove him to his knees to plead for release. God did not grant his request but gave him the grace to cope with the pressure.

The Bible tells us that Jesus went around doing good and — what?

....

....(Acts 10:38)

The end of this verse tells us that God was with Jesus. If we are "in Christ" we need have no fear of Satan because God is with us too.

What does James say will happen if we submit ourselves to God and resist the devil?

The devil will ....(Jas 4:7)

When we consider the terrible things that Satan does, we may wonder why the all-powerful God does not stop him. The problem is unlikely to be answered fully in this life. But we can consider the ways in which God uses the activities of Satan to fulfil His purposes.

25

B. God and the Problem of Evil

Since the world is controlled by the evil one, it is therefore a place where evil abounds. People are preoccupied with sensual pleasures and material possessions and their love for money results in all kinds of wickedness and suffering. Exploitation and injustice abound. The rich hoard their wealth and crush the poor. The planet's resources are plundered and abused, the rain forests are cut down and even the animals and birds — once named by man — are driven to extinction. The worst suffering is inflicted by man on his fellow man. Disease, famine and poverty reflect Satan's dark rule and awaken us to the nightmare of life without God.

What two things happen to people who pursue money?

....

....(1 Tim 6:10)

The Bible describes the last days as "terrible times" (2 Tim 3:1). Read 2 Timothy 3:1-5 to discover what people will be like.

There are a number of things that we can say regarding God and the problem of evil:

1. God allows suffering

God allows Satan's activity and man's sin to continue (Job 1 and 2). He also allows suffering in the world. The Bible does not explain all the reasons for this, but we must remember that God is Sovereign. He knows everything and we can be sure that everything He does is right and good.

Read Isaiah 45:9.
To whom does this "Woe" refer?"

....

26

2. God uses suffering

God has a purpose. He often accomplishes it without allowing pain. Good things happen to us, we rejoice and see Him establishing His Kingdom and bringing glory to His name.

But sometimes God chooses not to work in this way and instead accomplishes His purpose through suffering. He allows Satan and his demons to intrude; He permits sinful man to harass us; He locks us into difficult and painful circumstances.

In the Old Testament God's wrath against His enemies brought Him praise (Psalm 76:10). In the New Testament Jesus' enemies conspired together to do what God's "power and will had decided beforehand should happen" (Acts 4:28). Clearly no one will ever hinder Him from fulfilling what He has set out to do. He has decided that the church will make known His manifold wisdom to the rulers and authorities in the heavenly realms (see Ephesians 3:10). Let anyone try to stop Him!

Read Daniel 4:35.
What did the pagan king Nebuchadnezzar know about God?

....

....

....

How should we react to this?

....

3. God restrains evil

We can easily forget that God actually prevents evil from doing its worst (see 2 Thess 2:6-7). God has not abandoned this world. He loves it (John 3:16) and wants everyone saved (2 Peter 3:9). He has not brought everything to a speedy conclusion because He is patiently waiting for more people to become Christians. The church is involved with Him in this great commission. We declare the riches of God's grace to the world. We are the "salt of the earth".

How long ago did you become a Christian?

....

Aren't you grateful that God did not judge the world before you were saved?

4. God overcomes evil
The world is in Satan's control, but the Lord Jesus overcame him by His death on the cross (see 1 John 3:8; Col 2:15 and Heb 2:14). We therefore have authority over Satan through faith in Christ who delivers us from the power of sin and the fear of death. In His name we have authority over demons and sicknesses. We overcome by the blood of the Lamb and by the word of our testimony (Rev 12:11).

The victory is through faith alone. When we're going through difficulties, we believe by faith that God always works for our good (Rom 8:28) and that through Him we are "more than conquerors" (Rom 8:37). This is not triumphalism; we often fail, and we struggle with sin and with principalities and powers. Our ability to overcome with faith demonstrates that God's power is at work in us.

What did Jesus teach us to pray?

....

....(Matt 6:13)

Do you frequently pray this? YES/NO
Make it a daily habit from now on.

C. Sin and Suffering

Adam's rebellion against God had drastic consequences both for him and for us. Sin entered the world, and that sin separated us from God. It brought about spiritual death, more painful child-bearing, harder ground for man to work, murder, polygamy, immorality and idolatry.

Sin also brought sickness into the world. That is not to say that all sickness is the result of specific sin. Job certainly did not suffer because of sin. He was "blameless and upright" (Job 1:1). When Jesus' disciples asked Him, "Who sinned, this man or his parents, that he was born blind?" Jesus replied, "Neither" (see John 9:1-3). It is true to say, however, that sin can cause sickness.

Read Psalm 32:3-5.
What happened when David refused to acknowledge his sin?

....

....

D. God's Goodness and Love

It is wonderful to know the love and goodness of God. Love never seeks anything but the best for its object, and because God's character is perfect and good, He always deals with us in the right way. Just as the needle of a compass always points to the North so God is always good in all that He does.

Imagine a boat lost in the fog. The crew are at the mercy of the wind and waves, but they have a compass which tells them in which direction to steer. When we encounter trials and difficulties we need a reference point which is sure and certain. We can be absolutely confident that God is good. He always has been good and He always will be good.

Write out the first part of Psalm 119:68.

....

Read Psalm 145:17 and complete the following:

The Lord ....

and ....

Whatever may be happening to you at the moment, do you believe these statements about God? YES/NO

If we are ever tempted to doubt God's love and goodness, we need only look at the cross. Paul declares, "While we were still sinners, Christ died for us" (Rom 5:8), and John adds, "This is how we know what love is: Jesus Christ laid down His life for us" (1 John 3:16). The greatest sign of God's love for sinners came through suffering.

Fill in the gaps:
But because of His.. us, God, who is rich in mercy, made us alive with Christ... (Eph 2:4)

Read Romans 8:35-39.
Verse 35 mentions seven things that will not separate us from God's love. What are they?

....

....

When troubles come, the truth about God's goodness and love will keep you from being lost in a fog of doubt and uncertainty.

That happened to me on the day I was told about my incurable disease. Immediately I heard the news, I considered the goodness and love of God. The truth steadied me then and has kept me steady ever since.

Tick the statement which you think is correct:

☐ What we know should be governed by what we don't know.
☐ What we don't know should be governed by what we know.

When we lack revelation of truth we are vulnerable to attack. How Satan loves to undermine our trust in God so that we lash out at Him for what happens to us! Don't let Satan spoil your relationship with God! Rather, resist the devil, trust the word and put your confidence in an unchanging and faithful God.

E. God's Sovereignty

Acts 4 records one of the prayers of the early church when they were facing suffering and persecution. It begins, "Sovereign Lord..." (v 24). In the original Greek, this is expressed in one word, *despota* which means "absolute ruler". God is Sovereign, and He reigns over all creation. Those early followers of Jesus were totally convinced of God's sovereignty; it is a truth of which we too must be certain.

What three things does Paul say about God in 1 Timothy 6:15?

....

....

....

There are occasions when God puts up with evil men who are due for destruction in order to make known the riches of His glory to those who are being saved (see Rom 9:23-24). He can make a nation large or small (Obadiah 2). He can remove leaders of nations and raise up others in their place (see Psalm 75:7 and 1 Samuel 16:1). He can even use unbelieving leaders to serve his purpose and to bring good to His people. Three such individuals are Tiglath-Pileser (1 Chron 5:26), Cyrus (Is 45:1-7) and Artaxerxes (Ezra 7:21). They all pursued their own chosen course yet actually did God's sovereign will.

31

Poor Reflection

The apostle Paul tells us that until Jesus returns, our prophecies will be imperfect and our knowledge incomplete (1 Cor 13:9,10). One day we will understand everything, but for now we see only a poor reflection of the truth.

Trouble and suffering will certainly come. Our hearts will be broken and we will grieve over the distress of others. But whatever happens, we must remember that our God is a mighty Sovereign, One who reigns over everything. We are not serving our purposes in this generation. We are praying for God's kingdom to come and for His will to be done here on earth. Let's press on with faith, relying not on our reason, but on the infallible Word of God.

Chapter 3   DIFFERENT KINDS OF SUFFERING

Many people dismiss suffering as an experience that they have never had. Very few have endured severe hardships or pain. Most Christians have not been imprisoned or tortured for their faith. They have not faced famine, war or persecution by the state.

So what do we mean, when we talk about suffering? How does suffering come into our lives? Are there different kinds of suffering?

People can suffer in many different ways. All of us, have experienced suffering of one kind or another, although not all to the same degree or for the same length of time. If we look at some of the different kinds of suffering it will be easier for us to identify it in our own lives and also in the lives of others.

A. Physical Suffering
For most people this is the most obvious form of suffering because it tends to be visible or easily detectable. My own suffering has been mainly physical—I have had both extreme pain and severe disability. In addition to my main problem, an arthritic disease, I have encountered various unexpected extra difficulties. My skin is affected and I suffer from psoriasis and vitiligo (white patches on the skin). I have had pressure sores, ingrown toe nails, sensitive eyes, a collapsed lung, vertigo, and numerous kinds of infections. I know from experience that the body is one interconnecting unit. What happens to one part affects the others.

How can we cope with physical suffering? Besides pain killers what can we do to keep going?

Read Proverbs 18:14.
What helps a person to cope with physical suffering?

....

Our spiritual condition evidently has an important bearing on our ability to endure physical sickness. The Lord is able to strengthen our spirits and His grace is sufficient. Our Lord Jesus knows what physical suffering is like, so He can help us better than anyone else. We can also help ourselves.

Write down ways in which you think we can strengthen ourselves spiritually (eg meditation on the Word)

....

....

....

The Holy Spirit is our greatest source of strength and encouragement. Jesus told His disciples, "But the Counsellor, the Holy Spirit, whom the Father will send in my name, will teach you all things and will remind you of everything I have said to you" (John 14:26).

If you have never been baptised with the Holy Spirit, seek God about this experience. Maybe the immaturity or excesses of some Christians have kept you from receiving the Spirit and His gifts. But God's gifts are always good — even if some people use them badly. Why not find out more about it for yourself?

The Bible encourages us, "Eagerly desire spiritual gifts" (1 Cor 14:1). One of these gifts is "speaking in tongues" and Paul wanted all the Corinthians to use it (1 Cor 14:5). Many believers find that they are incapable of expressing to God, in words, what they feel in their hearts. But when we pray in tongues, we never have the problem of running out of words because the Spirit helps us.

34

So if you haven't written down, "speaking in tongues" in the exercise above, I recommend that you consider its importance. Tongues will enhance your prayer life and edify you. It is one of the most precious gifts that God has given us. We should be using it regularly.

What happens when we speak in tongues?

.... (1 Cor 14:4)

How does the Spirit intercede for the saints?

....(Rom 8:27)

What two things does Jude 20 encourage us to do?

....

....

Physically we may be weak, but spiritually we can know a fresh touch from God every day. The Bible has a lot to say about the spiritual renewal of Christians.

What comparison does Paul make between physical and spiritual well-being in 2 Corinthians 4:16?

....

....

What does David ask God to renew in him?

.... (Psalm 51:10)

What will be renewed if we hope in God?

....(Is 40:31)

It is very important for you to grasp this teaching — particularly if you are suffering physically. Often we spend more time being concerned about our bodies than we do about our spirits. Put your hope in God, read His word, ask Him to strengthen you inwardly, and you will find, as I have, that you can then cope with your physical problems.

Physical healing
What about healing? Should Christians be sick? Is it a lack of faith that prevents them being healed? There are so many questions like this, and so much confusion on the subject! I have met a great number of well-meaning Christians who have tried anything and everything to get me healed. Some have said my disease is demonic, others that it is caused by sin. I have been told that if I had more faith I would be healed. On odd occasions people have employed extreme measures. I've been pulled about, shouted at and rebuked — but all to no avail. What is the answer to this?

God does heal today! In spite of everything that has happened to me I have kept my heart from cynicism and scepticism. Most of the people who have prayed for me have been very loving, full of genuine faith and thoroughly biblical in their approach. They have invariably been Christians who know me. Although not healed, I have been strengthened and encouraged and have had a strong sense of God's presence. There is no doubt that I have been sustained by prayer and, at times, delivered from infections and other minor ailments.

To understand more about healing we must consider two key factors.

1. God's will
Some Christians think that sickness is not God's will. This viewpoint is difficult to uphold both from the Bible and from the experiences of many believers today. Paul's "thorn in the flesh" could have been a physical problem. If it was, it was not healed. Trophimus was left sick at Miletus (2 Tim 4:20). And Timothy was told to take wine for his stomach and "his frequent illnesses" (1 Tim 5:23).

It seems to me that we need revelation of the will of God for each situation. Jesus always acted in harmony with His Father's will (see John 5:19). Whenever He encountered people who needed physical healing He was sensitive to the leading of the Spirit. That's why we see Him healing people in different ways.

"The kingdom of God is not a matter or talk but of power" (1 Cor 4:20). Certainly God can heal and we must pray that He will do so. But we must also learn to be sensitive to the way that the Spirit is moving. Those who pray most effectively align their lives with God's Word and their requests with God's will (see 1 John 5:14,15).

2. God's timing
I am convinced that God will heal me! If you ask me why it hasn't happened yet, my reply is simply, "His time has not yet come." Ecclesiastes 3:3 says "There is a time to heal". I am waiting patiently for the Lord. My faith is growing stronger as I praise and glorify Him for His promises to me. I am confident that I shall see the goodness of the Lord in the land of the living (Psalm 27:13).

God always has a reason for withholding healing and we need to ask Him for revelation about this. If you are suffering physically, ask the Lord to show you what He wants you to do. He may reveal some hindrances to healing in your life (eg sin, lack of faith). If He exposes wrong attitudes, cynicism, unforgiveness or anger, deal with these things. He may then heal you, but if He does not, ask Him to sustain you.

B. Mental and Emotional Suffering
We live in times of great pressure and stress. One in three marriages ends in divorce, single-parent families are almost the norm, and young people are turning to drink and other means of escape because there seems to be nothing worth living for. Family break-up is traumatic for everyone involved, various phobias are on the increase and nervous exhaustion is becoming more common. Is it any wonder that a great

number of people are suffering mentally and emotionally, anxious and fearful about the affairs of life?

Christians too must contend with the pace and pressure of life. Many struggle daily with burdens which can, at times, seem unbearable. I encounter many anxious people, many who are hurt and some who are experiencing rejection. What does the Bible say about this kind of suffering?

1. Anxiety
What does Jesus tell you not to do?

....

....

....(Matt 6:25)

If we are experiencing financial pressures, we must learn to trust God for material things. Our heavenly Father knows our needs. He tells us to seek first His kingdom and righteousness, and promises that if we do this, all our needs will be supplied as well. Our minds must be set on things above and we must live a day at a time (Matt 6:33,34).

Read Philippians 4:6,7.
What does Paul tell us not to do?

....

What does he tell us to do?

....

....

....

....

What is the result?

....

....

....

Not only must we pray for what we need, we must also be thankful for the blessings that we already have. I often thank the Lord for His provisions and His grace. I can honestly say that I am thankful for all kinds of things, material and spiritual. This attitude of mind keeps us from being introspective and ungrateful. The Lord Jesus cares very deeply for us and does not want us to carry around worries which weigh us down.

What does the apostle Peter tell us to do with our anxieties?

....(1 Peter 5:7)

2. Hurts and rejection

The trouble with forming close relationships is that we get hurt and often feel rejected. Sometimes the problem is rejection by others; sometimes it is self-rejection. Jesus knows what it is to be rejected. He can heal rejection and also restore self-acceptance in our hearts. Because God has accepted us, we can accept ourselves.

Many Christians suffer from past hurts and need ongoing help from wise, Spirit-led counsellors. Others battle more with present-day hurts. They have to work through relationships with people who are close to them and that can be very painful.

Write down any hurts that you feel.

....

....

....

If these things are unresolved, pray about them and seek help if necessary. The key to dealing with hurt and rejection in our lives is to have a willingness to forgive those who have intentionally or unintentionally caused our hurt. It is no good holding grudges against people for what they have done to us in the past. We must find grace for the present.

When we encounter people who are hurting, we must remember that a crushed spirit is harder to bear than physical sickness (Prov 18:14). We must also distinguish between hurts that need healing and the hurt that people often feel when confronted by those who love them enough to tell them that they're wrong! The apostle Paul wrote a stern letter to the Corinthians and it hurt them, but they benefited from the sorrow they felt (see 2 Corinthians 7:8-10).

If you are feeling hurt or rejected: what is the reason for this?

....

....

How would Jesus react in your situation?

....

....

What are you going to do?

....

....

....

Those who suffer from physical or mental problems are not alone in their suffering. Their loved ones and friends experience the pain too. My wife shares all the troubles that I have. Sometimes it's worse for her because she sees me suffering. Caring for me certainly puts added strain on her and this makes it even more crucial for me to maintain my relationship with God and my spiritual health.

C. Difficult Circumstances

We must be careful that we don't bring problems on ourselves through lack of wisdom, or through disobedience to what God has told us to do. Jonah was a man who brought problems on himself. So watch out and don't be like him.

Having said that, people can suffer greatly from circumstances over which they have had no control and it is heartbreaking to see their sorrows and pains. Many of them experience problem after problem with little or no relief. Family relationships can bring worry, hurt and pressure. I've met many parents who have wept and grieved over the rebellion and waywardness of the children they love.

If you are going through family difficulties, remember that God is with you and that He cares for you and your loved ones. The most important thing you can do is pray every day for your relatives. The prayer of the righteous has great power in its effects. Don't give up and don't lose heart.

Racial prejudice also brings great suffering and stress. In this country ethnic minorities experience an undercurrent of resentment and hate towards them. I can identify with those who suffer because of racism since, as a disabled person, I too have known a type of prejudice. In the church there should be no class barriers and certainly no cultural barriers. Apartheid is rooted in man's heart and so is racial discrimination of any kind. Only the Gospel has the answer to this problem.

If you are feeling rejected or lonely because of your colour, then ask God to give you the grace to forgive those who have caused your suffering. Return good for evil and blessing for cursing. If you encounter prejudice within your local church, follow the biblical pattern for sorting out relationship problems (Matt 18:15-17).

There are other circumstances which affect our lives. Financial worries, job pressures and even church relationships can cause us problems. You may have smashed up your car, you may have a broken leg, there may have been a fire at home, you may be walking through the valley of the shadow of death. Whatever the cause of your suffering and difficulties, the Lord understands and He will comfort and strengthen you as you trust in Him.

It is right and good to receive from our elders, because their oversight and advice is an extension of the ministry of the Chief Shepherd to His people. Remember that you can go to Jesus direct because He is your Shepherd.

Whatever your circumstances, draw upon God's grace and goodness. People may let you down but the Lord cares for you and will never fail or forsake you. Let Him give you peace and restore your soul.

Read Psalm 23 and write out the verse that means the most to you at the moment.

....

....

....

D. Spiritual Attack

As Christians we can expect to suffer because of our faith and godliness. We must continually remember that we are engaged in a spiritual battle. Failure to do this will leave us vulnerable to attack, and will result in failure to take ground from the enemy. Satan is very active so we must be on our guard at all times.

Read 1 Peter 5:8, 9.
What must we do?

....

What is the devil doing?

....

What must we know?

....

....

Paul tells us that the devil schemes against us and that we fight not against flesh and blood but against demonic powers (Eph 6:11,12). If we are going to win the battle we must "be strong in the Lord and in His mighty power" (Eph 6:10). How do we do this?

We must stand together. In Ephesians 6, which concerns our putting on the armour of God, the words "you" and "your" are all in the plural. This emphasises the importance of our togetherness. Paul is addressing the Christian army, not just individuals. The church is made up of people who are closely related. We are described as "the body of Christ". A body has many interlinking parts. We are also described as "a building" which is founded on prophetic and apostolic foundations. The stones must fit together — each person plays a part in the whole.

We must be spiritually strong as individuals, but we must also be strong as an army which stands together against the powers of darkness. Together we must be righteous and full of faith. It is togetherness which will cause us to fulfil God's purposes locally and across the face of the earth.

Without reference to Ephesians 6:13-18, see if you can write down the different pieces of armour that we are told to put on.

1.. 4..

2.. 5..

3.. 6..

Now check your answers. Not only are we exhorted to put on the armour, we are also exhorted to pray. I am amazed that so many professing Christians treat prayer so casually. We should never miss a prayer meeting unless there is a good reason. We should be devoted to prayer!

Fill in the gaps:

And.................... in the...........................on.................................

with ....of .... and ....

With this in mind, ... for

...............the .... (Eph 6:18)

God is keen for us to pray. Does your favourite television programme take precedence over the prayer meeting? Do you let yourself off too easily? Next time you feel really tired and it's prayer meeting night, deny yourself, get there on time and get involved in prayer.

Read 2 Corinthians 10:4.
The weapons God has given us are not — what?

....

What do they have?

....

What do they do?

....

It is time for us to stop living the Christian life as if it were a holiday and to get into the battle! Like Paul, we must fight the fight of faith

(1 Tim 6:12). This means that we must be willing to suffer hardship and opposition as we advance and take ground from the enemy.

Fill in the gaps:

.... with us like a ....
of.................................   .... as a
.... gets involved in.. —
he wants to .... his ....(2 Tim 2:3,4)

E. The Christian and the World

Another major cause of our suffering as Christians is the ungodly world in which we live. Here we are not talking about the physical planet but about human society and the philosophies and politics which drive and control the people.

In the Bible the world and the church are portrayed in sharp contrast to each other. There is no neutral territory; people are either children of God or children of the devil (see 1 John 3:10). Those who don't know God are under Satan's evil rule and the world is Satan's sphere of influence (see 1 John 5:19). Jesus calls him the prince of this world (see John 12:31; 14:30).

Before we come to Christ we follow the course of this world (Eph 2:2) and live by this world's way of thinking and acting. But when we become Christians, we stop conforming to the world (Rom 12:2) and resist being contaminated by it (see Jas 1:27). Instead, we submit ourselves to God's rule which is righteous and just. Obviously we still live among people who are under Satan's rule and we have to resist the pressures that the world puts on us to conform to its philosophy and beliefs.

A good example of worldly thinking is the theory of evolution which leaves a Creator God totally out of the picture. Materialism is another strong influence that can affect our lives. No man can serve two masters, so you cannot serve God and materialism.

As Christians we will undoubtedly find ourselves at odds with the people around us. We have different values and our thinking is spiritual, not worldly. We recognise Satan's activity and the reality of sin. God's Word declares that men love darkness rather than light because their deeds are evil (see John 3:19). Since we are lights in the world, it will not be surprising when those who prefer darkness react adversely to us. We can expect hatred and persecution. It is a sobering thought that more Christians have been martyred in this century than in all the other centuries before it.

Just as a boat must be in the water, but the water must not be in the boat, so we are in the world, but the world must not be in us!

What did Jesus pray for us?

....

....

.... (John 17:15)

Godly people often generate adverse reaction from ungodly people. We must expect to experience persecution and hardship for the sake of the gospel. We are like sheep in the midst of wolves!

Read John 15:19.
Why does the world hate us?

....

Jesus has sent us into the world (see Matt 28:19 and John 17:18), but He does not want us to love the world or the things in the world.

Read 1 John 2:16.
What three things does John identify as coming from the world?

....

....

....

A great task has been set before us: we must preach the gospel of the kingdom to the whole world and then the end will come (see Matt 24:14). To fulfil this great commission, we must be prepared to suffer and to endure hardship. We must return blessing for cursing, good for evil, and love for hate.

Are you a good soldier of Christ Jesus? Are you free from the entanglements of this world? Are you building yourself up spiritually? Do you pray at all times in the Spirit? Are you preoccupied with your problems, or are you serving the purpose of God and preoccupied with His will? Be strong in the grace of God and let Him strengthen you and establish you in your Christian life. Peter says that:

"The God of all grace, who called you to His eternal glory in Christ, after you have suffered a little while, will Himself restore you and make you strong, firm and steadfast. To Him be the power for ever and ever. Amen" (1 Pet 5:10,11).

We have already established the fact that, as Christians, we will face problems and difficulties in this world. We have already looked at some of the troubles that we will encounter. But, thankfully, there is more to the Christian life than hardship and suffering. There are lots of blessings and benefits for us to experience as children of God and we can focus our attention on spiritual truths.

We have been saved from the wrath to come and have heavenly citizenship. We are "in Christ" and are righteous before God. We are part of God's family and have a perfect Father who loves us and supplies our needs. We have a purpose for living, a destiny to fulfil! Jesus is sending us on a mission — to proclaim the "good news" to the world.

It is good news of great joy, the most important news the world could ever hope to hear! What we have to say, will not just change people's lives, it will change their standing before God and will determine where they go in eternity. If you have the Son you have life, and when the Son sets you free, you are free indeed! The world sings about freedom and craves immortality, love and peace. We have them all!

The Bible describes people in the world as being "without hope and without God" (Eph 2:12). We have both. But sadly, looking at many Christians, you wouldn't believe it! They somehow fail to grasp the glorious truth of their standing in Christ and instead have a kind of mediocre existence on the earth.

The world clings to a "here and now" mentality. Those who don't know Christ cannot accept or understand spiritual realities (see

1 Cor 2:14). They are bound to this present age which is going nowhere. The Bible tells us that the wisdom of this world and the rulers of this age will all come to nothing.

The Corinthian believers were earthbound in their ways.
Read 1 Corinthians 3:1,3.
How did Paul describe them?

....

What were they doing?

....

....

Unlike the world, we are able to receive spiritual truth. The Spirit searches the deep things of God, knows the thoughts of God, and enables us to understand what God has freely given us. As citizens of heaven it should be natural for us to adopt a heavenly perspective. This is vital where all aspects of life are concerned, but it is especially important with regard to problems and suffering.

The Holy Spirit is in us. He is the teacher who helps us to know and understand spiritual things (see 1 John 2:27). Without Him, we would be incapable of getting a spiritual perspective on suffering, and we would have no concept of the life to come or the eternal nature of the unseen realities which God has promised us.

If you are earthbound in your thinking you must allow the Spirit to give you an eternal perspective on this life and its problems. Let God continually fill you with the Spirit and ask Him to bring revelation to your heart.

Read 2 Corinthians 4:17,18 and answer the following:
How does Paul describe our troubles?

.... and ....

What are they achieving for us?

....

....

What must we not fix our eyes on?

....

What must we fix our eyes on?

....

What is the difference between the two?

....

When we view things with an eternal perspective, the present troubles are overshadowed by something far greater which is yet to come. Are you spiritual in your thinking? Dr Martyn Lloyd-Jones said, "There is a difference between rational thinking and spiritual thinking. Rational thinking is not spiritual. Spiritual thinking is not irrational."[1]

God wants us to look spiritually at life and its problems. This is one of the major reasons why I can cope well with being in a wheelchair. I have a spiritual perspective on my situation. If I looked rationally at my disability, I would probably become depressed very quickly. As it is, I am confident that the Lord will fulfil His purpose for me and He will eventually bring me to glory!

Read Romans 8:28. Do you love God?   YES/NO
Have you been called according to His purpose?   YES/NO
What can you know?

....

....

....

This truth alone should change your perspective on the things that happen to you. As Christians we "live by faith, not by sight" (2 Cor 5:7).

We must keep our eyes on Jesus (Heb 12:1,2) and lay up treasure in heaven, not on earth. Jesus said that the position of our treasure will determine the location of our hearts (Matt 6:21). Where is your treasure?

Be honest with yourself and write down the things that you treasure most (eg a possession, a book, a relationship, a job, the Bible, a hobby, prayer...).

....

....

....

....

....

Now judge for yourself whether you are spiritual or worldly.

Is your heart divided, or are you earnestly seeking God's kingdom above everything else? Do you have an eternal perspective? Do you look rationally or spiritually at things that happen to you?

Here are some examples of rational and spiritual thinking:

Rational thinking	Spiritual thinking
I've got an incurable disease, my life is ruined and there is nothing worth living for.	I've got an incurable disease but I know God is in control of my life. I belong to Him and I know He will fulfil His purpose for me.
We're short of money. We won't have any food at the end of this week. I won't be able to afford to tithe. How can I make some money?	I need not be anxious about our lack of money. I will pray about it and trust God to supply our needs. The Lord can teach us to trust Him through this experience.
I'm worried because I might lose my job. How would we live? How would we pay the mortgage? I won't get another job if I lose this one.	The Lord is with me even at work. I know that whatever happens to me He will watch over me and my family. If I lose my job I can trust Him to give me another. Whatever happens I won't be afraid because God is working for my good in everything.
How can I know the right person to marry? My marriage could fail — so many end in divorce these days.	I'm praying about a partner in life. I know that God will lead me to the right person and I will wait patiently for God's plan to unfold.

Consider your own situation and write down a rational way of thinking about it. Then consider how God wants you to view it and write that down too.

Rational thinking

....

....

....

....

Spiritual thinking

....

....

....

....

Take to heart what you have written.

A. Stand Firm

If our perspective is right we can trust God, whatever happens to us. When we don't understand what's going on, we can still know that He is working for our good. It is tragic to see Christians go through suffering and begin to doubt that God loves them. It will not be long before they begin to feel angry and resentful towards God and others.

Satan makes the most of every opportunity he can find to turn our hearts away from God. He jumps at any chance to drive a wedge between us and our heavenly Father. We must not be ignorant of his devices. He is a liar and the father of lies (John 8:44). Don't let him undermine your confidence and trust in God. Stand firm in the Lord and hold onto the truth of His word.

Jesus went through temptation in the wilderness.
Read Matthew 3:17 and 4:3.
What was the devil trying to do?

....

There is one phrase in Matthew 4:1-11 that occurs twice. It precedes Satan's first two temptations. What is it?

....

Jesus used the Word of God to withstand Satan's attack. We must spend time in the Scriptures. It's good to read books and listen to tapes, but they are no substitute for the inspired Word of God. We are exhorted, "Let the word of Christ dwell in you richly" (Col 3:16). Only the sword of the Spirit will defeat the evil one. Let the Bible shape your perspective on life and eternity, and let it form your concept of God and His character.

According to Jesus, how will the Word affect us?

....(John 17:17)

B. People with Spiritual Perspective
As we read the Bible we come across different individuals who received revelation from God about their circumstances. Often this revelation came after prayer, and it brought a new perspective to the events which were taking place. Let's look at some of the characters concerned.

1. Joseph
Joseph was put in a pit, sold as a slave and imprisoned for something he didn't do. But God vindicated him and he became Pharaoh's right-hand man. After the death of Jacob, Joseph's brothers were afraid that Joseph would take revenge on them for treating him so badly. Read Genesis 50:19,20.
What was the brothers' original intention?

....

What was God's intention?

....

What was accomplished?

....

(see also Genesis 45:5-9)

Joseph brought God into the picture. In prison, Joseph couldn't see the complete plan, but as ruler of the land, he could see how God had arranged his circumstances. That's why he held no bitterness towards his brothers, or resentment towards the God who was watching over his life.

2. Rebekah

Isaac prayed for his wife Rebekah who was barren. The Lord answered his prayer and she became pregnant with twins. When the two babies began to jostle each other in her womb, she exclaimed, "Why is this happening to me?"

What did she do then?

....(Gen 25:22)

What was she told?

....(Rom 9:12)

This is an example of God's sovereign choice of an individual. When, like Rebekah, you don't know what is happening to you, it is good to seek the Lord for enlightenment.

3. David

In Psalm 132:1 we read, "O Lord, remember David and all the hardships he endured". David obviously went through a lot of difficulties. But what perspective did he have on them?

Read Psalm 119:67. What did he do before he was afflicted?

....

What does he do now?

....

Read Psalm 119:71. What does he say about his affliction?

....

56

What was its purpose?

....

Read Psalm 119:75. What does he say about God's laws?

....

What does he say about God's treatment of him?

....

4. Paul
The apostle Paul received an abundance of revelations, but his life was not problem-free. He was tormented by a "thorn in the flesh" which he prayed might go away. It did not. God had given him the thorn to keep him from becoming conceited about his revelations. He had to learn that God's grace is sufficient.

When Paul realised that his weakness would be used to glorify God, his perspective changed completely and he saw his problems in a totally new light.

How did he react to weaknesses, insults, hardships, persecutions and difficulties?

....

(see 2 Corinthians 1:8 and 9)
It is very important to remember that God's power is made perfect in weakness and that when we are weak we are strong (2 Cor 12:9,10). God sometimes allows us to go through difficulties so that we can bring more glory to Him and be greater channels of His grace and power. He wants us to rely on Him at all times. Without Him we can do nothing; with Him we can do all things (Phil 4:13).

C. Perplexity
When we don't understand the situations and circumstances surrounding us we become perplexed. In itself perplexity is not sinful,

but it can open the door to frustration, temptation, and even despair. We conquer perplexity by having a spiritual perspective.

Asaph was perplexed. He saw the wicked prospering, envied them and almost lost his foothold (Psalm 73:2,3).

In your own words, explain what was happening to Asaph while the wicked were thriving.

....

....

....

....(Psalm 73:13,14)

When we feel perplexed it is unwise to speak negatively as this could discourage and undermine the faith of others (see verse 15). The book of Proverbs tells us that "The tongue has the power of life and death" (Prov 18:21). So when you're going through a difficult time, consider the consequences of what you say.

This does not mean that we never share our problems and fears with others. We need fellowship during difficult times and we can derive wisdom and strength from those we love and trust in the Lord. The crucial issue lies in the attitude of our hearts. If we are requesting prayer from our friends or are in a counselling context, we should speak honestly about our problems. But if, while we speak casually to people, we are merely venting our anger, we can adversely affect them. If our trust in God is steady and our hearts are at peace, sharing our weaknesses or doubts can actually encourage others.

Asaph's problem is resolved when he gets a true perspective on the wicked people he has envied.

Read Psalm 73:16-19.

In your own words, what will happen to those who are ignoring and disobeying God?

....

....

....

When we meet with God's people, we should expect God to speak to us. The church is God's building, His dwelling-place. The wicked will one day be judged for their words and actions but the righteous will live in the presence of God for ever.

In the end this man could say that God was the strength of his life. He knew that God was near and that one day He would take him into glory. Such confidence is the birthright of all God's children.

D. Things to Guard Against
When we encounter problems we must guard against...

1. Self-pity
In the face of trouble, we can easily start to feel sorry for ourselves. Self-pity leads to bondage. It will cause you to feel "hard done by" and unloved. It's one of the devil's most subtle and deadly weapons.

2. Worry
We have already looked at the problem of worry and anxiety in Chapter 3. Here are the important principles which will help you guard against them:

a) Pray about everything (Phil 4:6).
b) Live a day at a time (Matt 6:34).
c) Let Jesus take your worries (1 Peter 5:7).

As you trust God and give thanks to Him, God's peace will guard your heart and mind in Christ Jesus.

3. Anger

Paul says, "in your anger do not sin" (Eph 4:26a). There is room for righteous anger (eg against injustice). But if we're not careful, anger can spill over into sin. In times of stress, or pain, we can easily get angry with people around us and even with God. We end up in a terrible state. Paul tells us not to let the sun go down while we are still angry (see Eph 4:26b). Clearly we must deal with relationship problems on a daily basis. We must also maintain our faith in the love and goodness of our heavenly Father. Don't let Satan get a foothold in your life by allowing anger to have its horrible way.

4. Self-neglect

During difficult times we often lose the desire to pray or read God's word. We therefore neglect ourselves spiritually. We must not allow this to happen. Rather, we must regularly meet with God and spend time speaking in tongues. The Spirit will help us to pray and tongues will edify us (1 Cor 14:4). We must also continue to meet with other Christians. When some people experience problems they stop going to meetings at their local church. We must not miss opportunities to meet with other believers (Heb 10:25). It is at times of difficulty when we most need the strength and encouragement that brothers and sisters in Christ can give.

5. Fear

Problems can produce fear. We can fear pain, the devil or rejection by others. Some people are afraid of what the future will bring. Others fear for their well-being in the present. God has not given us a spirit of fear (see 2 Tim 1:7). Paul confessed to "fears within" (2 Cor 7:5) but God comforted him through the visit of Titus. Heart-relationships are very important, not least when we hit hard times! The one certain cure for our fear is the perfect love of God (1 John 4:18).

6. Wrong-speaking

Paul says, "Do not let any unwholesome talk come out of your mouths, but only what is helpful for building others up according to their needs, that it may benefit those who listen" (Eph 4:29). If every Christian obeyed this teaching the church would be transformed overnight! Gone would be all grumbling, criticism, gossip and innuendo.

7. Self-centredness
Since we get obsessed with our problems and needs, we can very easily focus all our attention on ourselves. To be blunt, self-centred people are a pain! It's one thing to be in pain but you don't have to be one! If you are suffering, try loving others with the love of Jesus. "Agape" is a self-giving love. This will cause you to focus all your attention on others instead of yourself.

8. Moaning and grumbling
It's amazing how many Christians have formed the habit of moaning about things. They moan about the leadership, about the meetings and about their problems.

The Bible says that we should do all things without grumbling (Phil 2:14). Resist this awful habit as much as you can! Ask those closest to you if you moan a lot. If the answer is "Yes" then change and start encouraging and affirming those around you. (see 1 Cor 10:10; Jas 5:9; and 1 Peter 4:9).

The Lord will help and sustain you as you face these different snares of the enemy.

E. Our Destiny
Philippians 3:20 reminds us that our citizenship is in heaven, that our destiny is glory, and that we are eagerly waiting for the return of our Lord Jesus who is coming back for His Bride, the Church.

The apostle Paul had a heavenly perspective which radically affected the way he lived. How did he live?

Fill in the gaps:

But one thing I do: .... what is .... and

.... what is ...., I ....

.... the............... to .... the .... for which

.... has .... me .... in ....

.... (Phil 3:13,14)

Let's make sure that we have a heavenly perspective and that our lives fulfil the purpose that God has for us. The things we see around us are temporary. This world will one day be burned with fire. But those who do the will of God shall live for ever (1 John 2:17).

The apostle Peter gives us this challenge:

"Since everything will be destroyed in this way, what kind of people ought you to be? You ought to live holy and godly lives as you look forward to the day of God and speed its coming. That day will bring about the destruction of the heavens by fire, and the elements will melt in the heat. But in keeping with his promise we are looking forward to a new heaven and a new earth, the home of righteousness" (2 Peter 3:11-13).

---

[1] Martyn Lloyd-Jones, Faith on Trial, IVP (1965), pp. 34-35. Used with permission.

Chapter 5   REJOICING IN SUFFERING

In Romans 5:1,2 Paul gives us three results of our justification. What are they?

a) We have........................... with God.

b) We have gained access into this .... in which we now stand.

c) We rejoice in the............... of the................of God.

These three things make us certain of our salvation. But there is something more that Paul wants to highlight. "Not only so" he says and continues...

Fill in the gaps:
...but we also ....in our ....because

we know that .... produces......................................;

....................................., ... and ....,

....................(vv3,4)

Christians do not react like unbelievers. They love their enemies. They see death as gain. And when they face difficulties, they don't grumble and complain, they rejoice! Only God can make them react like this.

His rule in our lives brings not only righteousness and peace, but also joy in the Holy Spirit (Rom 14:17). Rejoicing in suffering is one more result of our justification. It is the hallmark of genuine children of God. Don't worry, if you have not been rejoicing in trials and difficulties. It does not mean that you're not saved! But it is possible for you to rejoice, and it is God's will for you — even in the midst of suffering. This teaching is not exclusive to the apostle Paul; it is found elsewhere in the New Testament. There are also references in the Old Testament which speak about the joy of God's people in the face of severe trials. Let's look at some of the key verses.

A. What the Bible Says about Rejoicing in Suffering

In the New Testament
Read Matthew 5:10-12. Why should we rejoice and be glad when we are persecuted?

....

Read James 1:2-4. Why should we rejoice when we face trials?

....

....

Read 1 Peter 4:12-14. Why should we rejoice when we face painful trials?

....

....

Jesus, James, Peter and Paul all teach that Christians should rejoice in times of suffering.

In the Old Testament
The prophet Habakkuk also brings this teaching. Read Habakkuk 3:17-19 and note down three of the calamities that he imagines could happen.

1...

2...

3... .

Write down three calamities that you fear could happen to you.

1...

2...

3...

Now write out for yourself Habakkuk 3:18.

....

In the time of Nehemiah the people stood, listened to God's law and mourned their sin. Their hearts were downcast and troubled. Then Nehemiah told them to go away and celebrate.

Fill in the gaps:

This day is .... to our .... Do not ....,

for the .... (Neh 8:10)

In films, the Lord is often portrayed as a very serious man. Jesus was, in fact, a very joyful person (see Heb 1:9). He was filled with a wonderful and lasting joy and must have had some great laughs with his disciples. It was for His bride, the church, that He gave Himself on the cross. That was the joy set before Him (see Heb 12:2).

Jesus wanted His followers to share His joy (see John 15:11). He's looking for individuals who are filled with inexpressible joy and a church that throws off its sombre outlook and overflows with gladness.

B. A Telephone Call with an Apostle
Have you ever wondered what it might have been like to talk to the apostle Paul? Let's imagine that you have been able to contact him on the telephone. How do you react to what he says?

Hello, Paul! Wonderful to hear you! How are you? **You're rejoicing!** Oh good! You've been preaching the gospel everywhere? Great! How did things go at Philippi? You had a few problems? What sort of problems? You were put in prison! Paul that's terrible. What happened? You healed a slave girl... they flogged you... put you in the stocks... and you were stinging? Oh — you were singing! I bet that brought the house down! You and Silas were **rejoicing** because you were suffering for Jesus. Paul, you're amazing!

What's that? You've been doing some open-airs. But you had some problems with them as well? So have we. Last week our P.A. broke down! You were stoned! Paul that's terrible! You must have been very upset. What happened? You were preaching the gospel, the crowd turned nasty and started throwing stones? Paul that's really awful. How do you feel? **You're rejoicing!** You're going to do some more open-airs? Paul is that wise? You seem to be having such a bad time! Do try and look after yourself!

Shipwreck? What shipwreck? Paul I didn't know you were involved in a shipwreck! That's your third shipwreck! Paul, do you have to travel by boat? You must be devastated? You're not devastated. **You're rejoicing!**

Paul have you shared this with the brothers? What about Demas? What do you mean he's left you? What about the other brothers? They've left you too! Paul that's the worst thing that could possibly happen!

I know, we should rejoice in the Lord always. No you don't have to say it again, Paul! How can you rejoice at a time like this? I know Habakkuk did — but he was only short of figs and milk! You've been flogged, put in prison, stoned, shipwrecked three times and now all the brothers have left you. Things couldn't get any worse could they?

Thorn? What thorn? Paul have you been gardening again? I told you to stick to tent-making! Oh, it's not that kind of thorn. It's a problem. What sort of problem? A big problem! You can tell me what it is. No... really? That's terrible. Oh Paul! How do you feel about this terrible problem? **You're rejoicing!** His grace is sufficient for you? Paul you're incredible. God bless. Yes, I'll keep rejoicing! Bye.

C. The Reason

There is a reason why we can rejoice. It is because we know that sufferings produce something. Those two little words, "we know", are very important. What we know affects the way we live and the way we cope with and understand sufferings.

Complete the following verses:

Rom 8:28   We know that ....

....

....

Psalm 56:9   This I will know ....

John 11:42a   Father I knew that .... me

James 1:3   You know that ....

....

1 John 5:18   We know that ....

....

....

....

1 John 5:19   We know that ....

....

....

1 John 5:20a   We know also ....

....

....

....

....

We can rejoice because we know that suffering produces godliness and spiritual maturity in us. When we find ourselves in a crisis it's easy to forget that God is working for our good. We can also forget that our trials and problems are producing something of eternal value in our lives.

When King David felt downhearted, he spoke to himself, then he got a grip on himself.

Read Psalm 42:11. What did he say to himself?

....

....

What did he tell himself to do?

....

Of what was he confident?

....

We do well to follow David's example. There are times when we need to steady our hearts before God. It's not always a sign of madness to talk to yourself! We must be honest with ourselves about our feelings and meditate on God's word. If we don't get a spiritual foothold quickly, we will slip into depression and despair. The Holy Spirit is in us to help us and teach us all we need to know (1 John 2:27).

When you feel uncertain about what is happening in your life, hold on to things which you know to be true. You can be confident in the unchanging, enduring word of God and in the fact that God Himself never changes (Mal 3:6). Make up your mind to imitate Habakkuk and Paul — rejoice in the Lord! We can't be glad about the problems themselves, but we can always rejoice in the Lord (Phil 4:4) and in His unfailing love for us. So speak to yourself about these things. Your circumstances may be tough, but your problems will, if you let them, produce godliness and maturity in you.

D. Don't Misunderstand
What does Paul mean by the phrase, "We also rejoice in our sufferings" (Rom 5:3)? Is he saying that we should rejoice in pain for its own sake? Must we must keep a broad smile on our faces while singing continually, "I'm H.A.P.P.Y."? Somehow I don't think so! We are not being encouraged into stoicism! The Stoics were a Greek sect renowned for their ability to grit their teeth and endure hardship and suffering. God does not want a people who clench their teeth together and declare, "Praise the Lord anyway!"

But we are not being encouraged into masochism either! A masochist is someone who enjoys pain. Can you imagine Christians singing "More pain, Lord!" and crying, "Ouch, ouch that's great! Oh, how I love it!"?

No, what Paul means is that we must rejoice "on account of" our sufferings. We know that God is at work in our lives. We know too that our sufferings are temporary and that they will build our character. That is why we can rejoice.

There is a subtle difference between joy and happiness. Happiness is dependent on circumstances but joy is not. Paul was often unhappy with his circumstances. He says he is "sorrowful". But then he adds, "yet always rejoicing" (2 Cor 6:10).

E. Now and For Ever
Since 1977, I can truly say that I have been able to rejoice "on account of" my disease and the resulting disability. The joy of the Lord has been my strength and I shall continue to rejoice in Him.

Are you rejoicing? How do you cope with problems, pain and

persecution? Do you quickly lose your joy over even the smallest thing? How do you react when you run out of milk; when the tape player won't work; when you get a cold or when someone is rude to you? Do you get angry and upset?

Pray for grace to help you in time of need. Recognise that God is working out His purpose in your life and rejoice. Your suffering will not go on for ever.

Look up Isaiah 35:10 and fill in the gaps:

and the .... of the Lord will return. They will enter Zion

with.............................; everlasting................. will crown their heads.

...................................and ....will overtake them,

and .... and .... will flee away.

Chapter 6   NEVER GIVE UP

After fourteen years of physical illness I thought I knew what endurance was all about. I reckoned that I'd exercised enough to last a lifetime! But God evidently thought that there was room for improvement. I'm glad that we don't always know what's in store for us!

Towards the end of 1990 I had what I thought was a routine x-ray and ended up in hospital for two weeks. My lung had collapsed and there was air trapped between it and its lining. A pipe was inserted into my side to release the air. In the next few months my lung collapsed five times which meant that I had to have five drains and then a general anaesthetic so that the lung and its lining could be stuck together. On one occasion I thought I was going to die so I wrote my wife a farewell letter and left it among my belongings.

The amazing thing is that the Lord gave me incredible peace and joy during that difficult time. I was given grace to bear the needles and the cuts in my side. But even more important, I was able to endure the trauma of not knowing what was going to happen to me. One minute I thought that God had healed my lung and the next minute it had collapsed again. I was suffering in the dark. There seemed to be no reason why these things were happening to me.

Maybe you are having to endure something like this. Let me encourage you — don't give up, and don't overlook the value of endurance. I have been waiting a long time for God to heal me and sometimes my condition seems to be getting worse rather than better. But in spite of perplexity and pain I have learned to keep going and to keep trusting.

You can't learn endurance if you have nothing to endure! Sufferings produce endurance. So instead of giving up in the face of severe trials, we put our trust in God and His Word, and we keep going. This is faith in action. As James says, "I will show you my faith by what I do" (Jas 2:18).

Endurance is a key Christian quality. There are no short cuts to it. You have to suffer in one way or another. But once you have learned to endure, you will have a spiritual maturity which will manifest itself in a number of different ways.

Write down what you consider to be the marks of Christian maturity (eg stability, discipline, commitment).

....

....

....

....

Without looking at James 1:2-4, put these six phrases in the right order by numbering which should go first, second etc.

Number
... because you know that the testing of your faith
        develops perseverance
... whenever you face trials of many kinds
... not lacking anything
... perseverance must finish its work
... consider it pure joy
... so that you may be mature and complete

Now check your answer.

This is how J.B. Phillips translates these verses:

"When all kinds of trials and temptations crowd into your lives, my brothers, don't resent them as intruders, but welcome them as friends! Realise that they come to test your faith and to produce in you the quality of endurance. But let the process go on until that endurance is fully developed and you will find you have become men of mature character, men of integrity, men with no weak spots." [1]

The path to godly character and maturity is through suffering. When our heavenly Father allows us to experience hardships and difficulties He is testing our faith and our dependence on Him for grace and strength. His power is made perfect in our weakness. As we go through trials we will feel totally inadequate, weak and drained. But when we are weak, we are strong!

Read 2 Corinthians 4:6,7.
Why is the treasure in "jars of clay"?

....

....

A. Great Endurance
Paul said to the Corinthians, "We commend ourselves in every way: in great endurance..." (2 Cor 6:4). Endurance was certainly a characteristic of his life. He went through the most incredible trials.

From memory, write down the difficulties and dangers he faced. (I've given you some hints.) Those you can't recall, look up in 2 Corinthians 11:24-26.

Five times I received ... the f...

Three times I was b...

Once I was s...

Three times I was s..

I spent a n...

I have been c..

I have been in danger from r..

in danger from b..

in danger from m...

in danger from G...

in danger in the c..

in danger in the c..

in danger at s...

in danger from f..

Paul was the original "Danger Man"! But the list is not yet complete. Read 2 Corinthians 11:27,28 and jot down briefly what else he had to endure.

....

....

....(see 2 Cor 6:4-10)

Hands up anyone who wants to be an apostle! Paul had to endure the most amazing pressures, but he pushed through by the grace of God and fulfilled God's purpose for his life.

Few of us have experienced the kind of hardships that Paul did. But I can't help feeling that if our zeal for the Gospel were equal to his, we would encounter a lot more suffering and persecution. Most of us are enduring inner struggles and fears, or difficulties connected with our personal lives. The Israelites struggled with these things in the desert. They had to overcome immorality, idolatry, fear, unbelief, and rebellion. It was only when they crossed the Jordan that they really started fighting battles for the glory of God — driving out the ungodly nations and taking possession of the land.

Their early mistakes are a warning to us. We can focus too much on ourselves rather than on the establishment of the kingdom of God. We have a message to proclaim to the nations. God wants us to know Him, the power of His resurrection and the fellowship of His sufferings. We must break out of the wilderness of shallow, lukewarm Christianity and give ourselves wholeheartedly to fulfilling the purpose of God in our lives.

Paul is a great example for us. He's just like us — weak and vulnerable — but he's sold out for God. He's in constant danger, he's often in prison, he dices with death, but he keeps going.

Remember, this is the man who wrote, "we rejoice in our sufferings" and, "rejoice in the Lord always". Paul didn't have an easy time and yet he was always rejoicing and trusting in the Lord.

B. Patient Endurance
God's people are characterised by rejoicing in suffering and by endurance. The difficulties we face will call for — what?

....and...............................(Rev 13:10 & 14:12)

Where is the source of this?

....(Rev 1:9)

James tells us that the prophets are an example of patient endurance (Jas 5:10). Prophets are a rare breed who have to endure special hardships. They receive revelation before everyone else and therefore live with the frustration of knowing what others have not seen. They have to learn to be patient with God's people and to endure the frustration of waiting longer than anyone else to see God's purposes fulfilled.

James also points out Job as an example of patient suffering (Jas 5:11). He endured terrible trials, yet he kept trusting God, and God vindicated him. Like me, you may be going through great difficulties. Take heart! Just as we know the end of Job's story, so God knows the end of ours. Who knows what He is planning to do for you? You are blessed if you persevere (Jas 5:11).

Paul said to the Corinthians, "If we are distressed, it is for your comfort and salvation; if we are comforted, it is for your comfort, which produces in you patient endurance of the same sufferings we suffer" (2 Cor 1:6).

Our heavenly Father is the "God of all comfort" (2 Cor 1:3). Paul and his companions received God's comfort in their sufferings and were able to impart that comfort to the believers in Corinth. When the Corinthians were comforted, they were able to endure patiently what was happening to them.

Sometimes we may face hardships beyond our ability to endure (see 2 Cor 1:8) but God will give us the strength we need to overcome (see Rom 15:5).

Jesus commended the Ephesian Christians for their perseverance and the believers in Philadelphia for keeping His command to endure patiently (Rev 2:3; 3:10). Churches, as well as individuals, need patience as they wait for the restoration of the church. The church takes time to build. We are God's co-labourers and we shall find that things do not happen as quickly as we should like or in the way we want them to. At all times we must be committed to God's vision for His church, maintain our zeal, keep the unity of the Spirit and be patient.

I'm waiting patiently for God to heal me. Over the past few years, thirty individuals have approached me separately and have shared the same dream. Each one saw me standing up straight, totally healed. Prophecies and revelation to my own heart have also pointed very definitely to a complete healing. I have no doubt that when God's time is right, He will act. But right now life is tough. I'm learning to endure and to wait patiently for the Lord. I'm trusting Him and serving Him with all my heart.

Patience is a fruit of the Spirit. Are you enduring with patience? Ask God to help you do so.

Fill in the gaps:

May the Lord direct your ....into............................

and... (2 Thess 3:5)

C. Genuine Faith

Genuine faith continues under trial. This is one of the most important truths we can learn. Jesus once said, "he who endures to the end will be saved". That is not to say that salvation is the reward for endurance but rather that endurance is the hallmark of salvation.

Dr Martyn Lloyd-Jones says:
"There is no more important and no more subtle test of our profession of the Christian faith than the way we react to the trials and the troubles, and the tribulations of life in this world. There is no test that is more delicate, more sensitive, than this particular test. I have sometimes ventured to describe it as the acid test of a man's profession of the Christian faith." [2]

So problems and hardships test the authenticity of our faith.

Read 1 Peter 1:7. What is your faith worth?

....

If your faith is proved genuine, what is the result?

....

....

True faith is able to endure trials and problems and involves more than just a mental assent to the Gospel. It requires true repentance which leads to a whole new lifestyle. The Gospel we proclaim is not merely to do with our personal experience of God. It is essentially what God has done in time and history in sending His Son to die on the Cross. People need to be born again, not simply persuaded to add a bit of Christian belief to their present lifestyle.

Most unbelievers will readily admit that they'd like more joy and peace, and often look favourably on "religious experiences". But unless we're careful, we can persuade them to add a bit of Christian belief to all the other philosophies that are on offer to them. Instead of being born again, they remain unchanged within and display only an external form of godliness. They may clap and sing heartily in our meetings, but at the least sign of opposition or persecution, they fall away. They cannot cope with the demands of following Jesus. Hardship reveals that their faith is false.

In the parable of the sower Jesus speaks about the seed (God's Word) being sown in four different kinds of ground. These soils represent the conditions of people who hear the gospel. Some of the seed fell "on rocky places".

Read Matthew 13:20,21.
How does the man "on rocky places" receive the word of God?

....

78

Why doesn't he last long?

....

What makes him fall away?

....

This kind of person's faith is not genuine. The individual who merely has an emotional experience will not persevere when faced with difficulty.

You may have had many problems. If you have not fallen away, that proves that your faith is genuine! Be encouraged and keep going!

D. Keep your Eyes on Jesus
If we grow weary or feel tempted to grow weary and lose heart there is a sure and effective antidote: we consider Jesus.

Read Hebrews 12:2,3.
Why did Jesus show such a positive attitude towards His suffering?

....

....

What does this say to you about any suffering that you may face?

....

....

Jesus ran the race of suffering ahead of you. He gives you the strength to run and calls you to follow Him. Keep going! Sin can't dominate you any more because Jesus has set you free from its power. Don't let anything weigh you down or hold you back from living for God and serving His purpose for your life.

Be on your guard against apathy and lukewarmness. Suffering can make you lazy or half-hearted in your church commitments and in your Christian walk. Refuse to tolerate wrong attitudes in your heart or sin in your life. Be ruthless in dealing with unholy thoughts and selfish motives. We need to train ourselves in godliness and pursue such important things as righteousness, faith and love. Passivity will produce shallowness in your spiritual life, so be self-controlled and spiritually alert — whatever is happening to you.

If you endure ongoing or recurring problems, you must keep your eyes on Jesus. What does that mean in practice? It means spending time with God — praying and meditating on His word. I have gained much strength from the Bible during my long illness. You will discover the same. If you maintain your relationship with the Lord, you will be able to resist the solutions that the world offers you, and you will not neglect fellowship with other Christians. You will be able to rejoice too — because Jesus has overcome the world and because your trials are proving the genuineness of your faith.

E. The Challenge
Have you learned to endure hardship? Can you see the benefits of going through difficult circumstances?

Write down three things that you have had to endure

....

....

....

How have you changed as a result of enduring these problems?

....

....

....

What is God saying to you about patience in suffering?

....

....

....

If you are impatient and easily discouraged, ask God to help you change.

Get a new perspective on things that are happening to you and trust God to do a new work of grace in your life.

Don't lose heart when you pray! Keep asking, seeking and knocking. You need endurance - God will give it to you (Rom 15:5,6).

---

[1] JB Phillips, *The New Testament in Modern English*, Revised edition, Harper Collins (1958).
[2] Martyn Lloyd-Jones, *Romans 5*, Banner of Truth (1971), p.60. Used by permission.

Chapter 7 KNOCKED INTO SHAPE

"Pain"! That's the word that comes to mind when we consider a visit to the dentist. It's incredible that we will actually pay to have somebody stick needles in our gums and drill our teeth. But why do we go? Because we know that in the long term we will be better off if we have regular dental treatment. The pain is for a purpose. The drilling deals with decay and turns deficient teeth into useful chompers again!

In the same way, hardship and pain produce in us godly and sin-resistant character. As Christians, we do sin and need forgiveness and cleansing but sin need not reign in our lives so that it becomes a regular habit (1 John 3:9). It is not impossible to sin, but it is possible not to sin! When we were born again we were given a new nature. Since that time the Holy Spirit has been helping us to conform to the image of Jesus. The apostle Paul talks about this process of change in the believer.

Fill in the gaps:

And we, who with ....all............................the

...., are being.. into his

.... with ....,

which comes from ...., who is the......................

(2 Cor 3:18)

Somebody once said that, before the world was made, God the Father looked at God the Son and wanted millions more like Him. He wants us like Jesus while we live (see Rom 8:29) and will make us like Jesus when we die or when He returns for us.

Unravel these words from 1 John 3:2:

> for appears be him we shall but see we know as that he shall
> when he is when we like

....

....

....

God wants to sanctify us through and through so that at our Lord's
coming we may be found blameless in spirit, soul and body (1 Thess
5:23).

Endurance sharpens our resolve to live for God and develops our
spiritual muscles. We look beyond the desires of our flesh and seek
to live for the glory of God.

Some years ago we used to sing a chorus called "Jesus is changing
me". There was one part that I've never forgotten. It went like this:

> Jesus is changing me, hallelujah!
> Jesus is changing me
> The work of the refiner's fire
> To be as pure gold
> In the house of the Lord
> To bring right offerings to Him [1]

We often sing songs without realising the full implications of the
words. It may be that many of us don't see the need for change or for
the problems and pain in our lives. But God is at work in us, not to do
what we think is best, but "to will and to act according to His good
purpose" (Phil 2:13). He is refining us and making us like "pure gold".

Read Job 23:10. What was Job sure that God knew?

....

What was God doing?

....

What would be the result?

....

Can you say the same? YES/NO

God allows us to go through difficult times, so that we can learn to endure. This has the effect of maturing and refining us.

Charles Swindoll says:

"God is more concerned with our character than with our comfort. His aim is not to pamper us physically, but to perfect us spiritually." [2]

Even Jesus discovered the importance of endurance.
Complete this verse from Hebrews 5:8:

Although He was a Son, ...

....

Jesus was sinless and yet He willingly submitted to the same maturing process that we must endure and lived in complete obedience to God. Because He was fully human, He went through human trials. He overcame genuine temptation and experienced real pain. He prayed about decisions and drew on His knowledge of the Word of God. He washed the disciples' feet, paid His taxes, and made sure that someone cared for His mother when the time came for His departure. He was faithful in everything and was obedient even to death (see Phil 2:8).

Jesus is our example. We must walk as He walked and love as He loved. His attitude must be our attitude, and we must endure as He endured.

So many Christians crave spiritual gifts and power more than Christlike character. Why? Because gifts are received whereas fruit must be cultivated and grown. We want the "instant" blessing but shy away from holiness and discipline because they're too costly.

What is God saying to you with regard to the development of your character? (eg He's challenging me about my unhelpful attitude to my parents)

....

....

....

....

What are you going to do about it?(eg I'm going to seek God's forgiveness for my unhelpful attitude to my parents, pray more for them and actively love them)

....

....

....

....

We long to see a greater manifestation of signs and wonders. God longs to see a holy people whom He can trust as channels of His power.

He knows that the best stewards are those of godly character; those who are responding to the Spirit and working at change; those who are getting on with the task and who are giving all the honour to Jesus.

A. Heart Condition
When gold is refined, all the dross comes to the surface. Similarly, when we go through difficult times, all the impurities in our hearts begin to reveal themselves.

When this happens, we are tempted to blame our circumstances for the way we are. The truth is that those circumstances are only bringing to light what is already there.

Write out Proverbs 27:19.

....

....

The heart is the centre of our emotions and will. What is in it will influence the way we live and what we say. No wonder Solomon exhorts us to — what?

.... (Prov 4:23a)

Why?

....(Prov 4:23b)

Character weaknesses have destroyed many gifted ministries. Just as the gifts of the Spirit are useless without love (1 Corinthians 13), so a gifted ministry within the church is of no value without godly character to harness and direct it.

If you want to be a channel of God's love and power, you must have a pure heart. During times of stress or pain God will reveal to you the true condition of your heart and show you where your weaknesses are. When this happens, don't resist Him. Face up to the truth and deal with anything that He shows you.

Read Psalm 139:23,24 and fill in the gaps:

......................................, O God, and ....

....and ....

....

and ....

Pause and ask God to show you anything in your life that displeases Him. Write down anything that He shows you.

....

....

....

....

Do you examine yourself before breaking bread?
YES/NO/SOMETIMES

If the answer is not "YES" then you need to change your ways! God's word tells us to examine ourselves every time we break bread. We must obey this command because we need regular self-examination.

The fruit of the Spirit is:

..... love	..... patience	..... faithfulness
..... joy	..... goodness	..... gentleness
..... peace	..... kindness	..... self-control

Ask someone who knows you well to assess the extent to which these character qualities are evidenced in your life. They should work on a scale of 1-10. The lower numbers will suggest that you are lacking in certain qualities, the higher ones that you are excelling! Ask them to explain their reasons and work out how you can improve your lowest scores.

B. Motives and Attitudes
Deep in our hearts there are motives and attitudes that need to be refined. The Lord sees everything that we do and is fully aware of the motivation behind each action. The Bible says that He knows what we are going to say before we even open our mouths (Psalm 139:4).

Read Proverbs 16:2.
What is a man's reaction to "all his ways"?

....

What does God do?

....

Read 1 Corinthians 4:5.
When Jesus returns, what will He do?

....

....

....

One day every person's motives will be exposed. We must examine our actions in the light of this fact. So pause and ask yourself some searching questions. Why am I involved in that ministry in the church? Is it for the glory of God or for some other reason? Why do I sing/play in the worship group? Do I want to magnify His name or be admired by others? Why do I give money? Why do I contribute publicly to the Sunday meeting? Why am I writing a book? If we're honest, a lot of what we do is for mixed reasons, so all of us need to search our hearts and examine our motives. We must make sure that we are looking for praise from God alone.

Someone has said that motives are why we act the way we do, and attitudes why we react the way we do. The word "motive" comes from the same root as the word "motor". It's what drives us! Jesus taught His disciples about wrong motives in the Sermon on the Mount. He exposed the reasons why the Pharisees gave money, prayed and fasted.

What was their motivation?

....(Matt 6:2,5,16)

According to James, what happens when we pray with wrong motives?

.... (Jas 4:3)

Have you ever thought that this might be true of you? Wrong motives reveal weakness of character and a heart that is divided. According to 1 Corinthians 10:31, we should have only one motive. What is that?

....

....

We have looked at the motives — the underlying reasons why we do things. Now let's look at our attitudes — the way we react to things that happen. As ever, Jesus is our perfect example. We have already noted His obedience. Now we look at His attitude.

As the Son of God, He had every reason to seek honour from men. But He let go of the glory that rightfully belonged to Him and humbled Himself.

He submitted to His earthly parents, did only the Father's will and then laid down His life for us. As a result He is now exalted at the right hand of God and has a name that is above every name.

What does Philippians 2:5 say to us?

....

....

Throughout the years of severe pain, God has been dealing with the motives and attitudes in my heart. Regardless of what happens to me in the future, I want to fulfil His purpose for my life and glorify His name.

Whatever you may be enduring, let God change and refine you so that you live for His glory alone. Don't try to gain a reputation or seek an important role in the church. Don't try to be somebody. Rather, set your heart on God's will and have a right attitude concerning yourself and others. Don't allow envy or pride to take root in your heart. "God opposes the proud but gives grace to the humble" (Jas 4:6).

I remember watching my father-in-law hoeing in my garden. What puzzled me was that he seemed to be working over ground that was free of any weeds. When I asked him why he was doing this, he replied, "They always say you should hoe where you can't see the weeds. That way they can never take root!" This gardening tip made me think over the way I could keep my life free from wrong motives and attitudes. I must be vigilant so that no bad things can take root. Is there any envy or pride in my heart? Am I competitive or jealous? Am I driven by wrong ambitions? God wants me to seek Him about such things. He is the gardener. I must let Him uproot anything that resembles a weed and plant beautiful things in its place.

C. Loving Correction

As we encounter various trials, we must be careful to distinguish between spiritual attack and discipline from God. I've heard many Christians saying, "I'm under attack!" But I haven't heard many saying "I'm being disciplined!" There are times when spiritual attack and discipline from God seem to overlap. This is illustrated in Paul's experience with his "thorn in the flesh". It was clearly from Satan and yet the Lord used it to keep Paul from becoming proud. It is important to understand what is happening to us and why.

I always know when there is an unresolved issue between God and me. When trouble comes into my life at such a time, I am conscious that the Lord is allowing it in order to deal with my stubborn refusal to change or let go of something.

We must exercise honest self-appraisal and face up to things that God wants to correct in our lives. Spiritual attack is often clearly recognised and usually comes as we resolve to do God's will and live holy lives. If the attack is subtle, we obviously require greater discernment, but we need not be ignorant about Satan's devices. When we know that our hearts are pure and that sin has been confessed and cleansed we are better able to recognise and withstand spiritual onslaughts from the enemy.

The Bible tells us a number of important things about God's discipline. Read Hebrews 12:5,6.
What two things must we not do when God disciplines us?

....

....

Fill in the gaps:

because the Lord ....those He...............................

and He .... everyone He ....

When we go through trials we may be tempted to think that God hates us and is treating us like nobodies. In fact, the very reverse is true.

How are we encouraged to view hardship?

....

How is God treating us?

....

If we did not go through hardship, what should we assume?

....

Clearly God's correction is not evidence of rejection but proof of selection! God wants us to receive discipline, to endure it and to benefit from it.

Read Hebrews 12:11.
What does discipline feel like?

....

What is the result?

....

....

When our children were young we disciplined them — which sometimes meant that they received a loving smack. Now we are enjoying the good things that have resulted from that training. If discipline from a human father is so beneficial, how much more valuable is it from a perfect heavenly Father?! He chastens us for our good and wants us to share His holiness.

I once visited a home where a little boy was sick. He was lying on a couch and had to take his medicine while I was there. As he was about to swallow the red sticky-looking liquid, his mother asked him, "What does Daddy say?" He answered immediately, "The medicine that tastes the worst does you the most good!" I think that the painful experiences that God allows in our lives do us the most good. The medicine tastes horrible at the time but later on we're glad we took it.

We must understand that discipline is for our good, otherwise we will resent it. God is looking for people who will submit to His plan for their lives — even when it is hard. But more than that, He wants us to learn all we can from our situation and to give glory to His name.

D. Always Content
We have already seen how much the apostle Paul endured as he preached the gospel and served the churches for which he was responsible. In spite of his trials we never hear one word of resentment from his lips or see him flagging in his zeal for God. Regardless of his circumstances, he was always content.

Read Philippians 4:12 and fill in the gaps:

I know what it is to be ...., and I know what it is to

.... I have learned the secret of being.....................

...., whether................................. or

..............................., whether ....or in

....

Have you "learned the secret"? God wants you to be content, even during hard times. If you turn away from grumbling and moaning about difficulties, you will grow in your spiritual life and you will experience great peace — the sort of peace that gives you the ability to sleep in a boat through a storm! Your reaction to trials will prove that your faith is genuine.

Paul says, "Godliness with contentment is great gain" (1 Tim 6:6). Like endurance, contentment can be learned through experiencing difficult circumstances. If we have abundance for a long period of time God may take away our wealth to test our reaction to a simpler lifestyle. On the other hand, if we have not had much for a while, He may give us wealth to see if we can receive without feeling guilty. We must be so submitted to the will of God that we are able to adjust to our varied situations and yet maintain our complete trust in God.

Read Hebrews 13:5,6 and fill in the gaps:

Keep your lives ....and

.... with ...., because

God has said, "Never will I ....; never will I

......................................" So we say with confidence, "The Lord is

.... I will not be .... What can

...........................me?"

Many Christians are continually anxious and unsettled about their personal circumstances. Many others are preoccupied with accumulating worldly possessions. Both groups are distracted from fulfilling the purposes of God. We must not imitate either. Their actions prove their lack of faith in the promises of God. If we know that God will never abandon us, then let us be content no matter what happens to us. Let our actions continually prove our faith in His word.

---

[1] Alison Huntley, "Jesus is changing me". © 1978 Thankyou Music, PO Box 75, Eastbourne, East Sussex. Used by permission.
[2] Charles Swindoll, *Quest for Character*, Hodder and Stoughton (1987), p.81. Used by permission.

Chapter 8   REFINING RELATIONSHIPS

"You know that you asked me to speak into your life..." said a good friend of mine. "Well..." He was about to bring me some loving and wise correction following my contribution at a large meeting.

That morning, grace had not been abounding, it had been abandoned! In my opinion the assembled company had not been zealous enough in their worship, so I had decided to let them know about it. I challenged them hard and my words seemed to have the desired result. After I'd spoken people were dancing — even if they weren't smiling!

As soon as my friend spoke to me, I knew that reproof was on the way. It's true that I did ask him to speak into my life, but I never thought he'd do it! When he rebuked me I probably looked calm and submissive, but on the inside countless defence mechanisms were being triggered, like mines in a minefield.

It's so easy to invite others to speak into our lives. But when someone actually takes us up on our invitation, we don't like it one bit! We don't appreciate being told that what we have done is unhelpful.

In this case I realised that my reaction betrayed a wrong heart attitude and I received the criticism for my earlier behaviour. It was a struggle. Self never likes being strangled, and we are always tempted to justify ourselves. In the end, the discomfort did me good and I have since learned to accept reproof and correction from others!

In the church where I'm lead elder, there are six other elders working alongside me and they are not afraid to tell me the truth. They inform me when I waffle. They let me know if my sermons are too long, or boring. They reprimand me when I delegate one of them to lead a meeting and then take over myself. We love each other, and we are all friends. Our mutual openness and honesty is very healthy and I wouldn't have it any other way. We build each other up, correct each other and pray for each other. These relationships are refining us all and they help us to serve more effectively.

It may surprise you that a book about problems and sufferings should contain a chapter on relationships. Relationships are potentially a source of great blessing. They can have a beneficial effect on our character and conduct. But they can also be the cause of great pain. In our interaction with others we often find a lot of problems, complicated troubles and hurts. What others say and do to us can have a devastating effect on our lives. God is working out His purpose in all our relationships — relatives, friends and fellow Christians. He wants us to love, value and bless everyone with whom we come into contact.

The Bible has a lot to say about the refining that relationships bring into our lives.

Unravel these verses:

    love is better open than rebuke hidden

....(Prov 27:5)

    trusted be from can a friend wounds

....(Prov 27:6)

    is it a righteous head man on strike let me rebuke him
    let my kindness it is oil a me

....

....

....(Psalm 141:5)

We all need people who love us enough to tell us when we're wrong. When we begin "speaking the truth in love" we will really start to see the church grow. It will never function properly without such genuine and loving relationships.

The church is not just people, it is people who are joined in heart relationship. This means that we are bound to encounter pain and friction as we work together.

Write out Proverbs 27:17.

....

....

As God's people relate so the sparks fly! The hurts of honesty smooth away rough corners and true friendship emerges. Honesty doesn't damage friendship, it deepens it. A real friend will never give up on you and will always be available when needed.

Complete these two verses that underline this truth:

A friend...(Prov 17:17a)

There is a friend ....

....................................(Prov 18:24b)

Jesus brought out this truth when He said to His disciples, "You are my friends if you do what I command" (John 15:14). On this occasion, Jesus' friendship was not in question — He demonstrated that by laying down His life. Here He was scrutinising their friendship.

He was effectively telling them that a friend would always be faithful and have other's interests at heart. By their obedience, the disciples would demonstrate their faithfulness to Jesus and their love for Him (see John 14:15). Their friendship would be confirmed as real and lasting.

There are a number of occasions when Jesus found it necessary to rebuke His disciples. Admonition is one of the essential elements in the process of bringing people to spiritual maturity. It is something which also imparts wisdom and understanding.

A. The Results of Admonition

Read Colossians 1:28. What was Paul's goal?

That we may ....

How did Paul go about attaining this goal?

....

....

If we are going to be mature in Christ we need to be taught the word of God accurately and we need to be admonished and rebuked! Clearly elders will fulfil this role, but all of us will be involved because the Bible says that we can admonish one another (Col 3:16).

Compare Colossians 1:28 with Colossians 3:16. Where are the similarities?

....

....

....

Confrontation is never pleasant. Many who rebuke others actually can't take rebuke themselves, and many who regularly receive correction feel unqualified to correct others. We must guard our hearts from stubbornness and ultra-sensitivity — otherwise we will never grow spiritually.

There is always a need for accountability because no one is beyond correction. People in leadership are safeguarded when they are accountable to those who love them. On one occasion, Paul had to confront Peter about his reaction to the Gentiles (Gal 2:11-13). As an eldership we voluntarily submit both to one another and to apostolic ministry.

The book of Proverbs frequently refers to the need for admonition. Let's look at some of the results of it.

What does a discerning man gain from a rebuke?

....(19:25)

What is the benefit of listening to a life-giving rebuke?

....(15:31)

What is the result of rebuking a wise man?

....(9:8)

You would normally expect a rebuke to trigger an adverse reaction - regardless of the wisdom or discernment of the other person. But, according to God's word, this is not the case.

Complete these two Proverbs:

A rebuke ....
more than a hundred lashes a fool (17:10)

He who rebukes a man will in the end..
than he who has a flattering tongue (28:23)

Although reproof is often hard to receive, there is usually an awareness within the person being confronted, that the correction is justified. This has the effect of making him appreciate the truth and respect the one bringing the rebuke. Such honesty and faithfulness often form the foundation for permanent friendship.

Ben Davies wrote this in an article about confrontation:

"Lovingly speaking the truth to one another is the way friendships are deepened. Sometimes we may discover that a friendship isn't all it appeared to be. Confrontation will test our relationships but it is the route to establishing them in the love of Christ. Friendships that lack honesty will fail to produce the fruit of righteousness and will stunt spiritual growth. It is sad to see people who have become hardened and who lack openness to correction." [1]

Are you willing to receive rebuke and correction or do you react against them?

Are there any no-go areas that you have shut off from other people? Do you allow your God-appointed leaders to speak honestly to you (see Heb 13:17)?

Write down the names of three people whom you allow to correct you.

....

....

....

Have you received any admonition in the past? YES/NO
Outline any rebukes that you have recently received.

....

....

....

How did you respond?

....

....

....

How have you acted on the things that needed adjustment?

....

....

....

Guard against these three things:

❑ thinking you are always right;

❑ allowing past experiences (when you received unwise or unloving rebukes) to prevent you receiving correction now;

❑ covering up weaknesses or failures in your life (an unwillingness to be open and honest).

Tick the one(s) that ring true in your heart, pray about it/them and share the problem(s) with a mature Christian friend. When you can receive admonition you will, according to Proverbs, grow in wisdom and you will enjoy deeper relationships as well.

B. Made to Be Together

The Holy Spirit has continually emphasised the importance of shared lives and interdependence. The Bible provides us with pictures of togetherness: the body, with all its parts joined and working together, and the building, where living stones are built together into a dwelling place for God. But despite these strong images, many Christians still maintain their independence, run away from committed relationships, and only get involved with others on a very superficial level.

When the apostle Paul speaks about the Church as a body and as a building, he is emphasising our interdependence. We were created for relationship! On our own, we will never become mature Christians.

What can't we say to each other?

....(1 Cor 12:21)

We need one another. We need to be provoked by others who are living to please God. We need to share our possessions (Heb 13:16), bear one another's burdens (Gal 6:2) and confront one another in love. As we work out our relationships, we will inevitably get hurt, but the pain will be thoroughly worthwhile. God will refine our lives and we will begin to function more effectively together.

This matter of interdependence is relevant to the whole question of suffering in that God does not want any of us to suffer in isolation.

Write out the first part of 1 Corinthians 12:26.

....

....

To ensure that this quality of relationship is being worked out on a practical level, we must not be meeting-oriented. Jesus did not say, "I have come that you may have meetings, and have them more abundantly!" We can attend lots of meetings and yet still be desperately lonely. Our focus must, instead, be on cultivating the kind of friendship and love that makes a visiting stranger feel wonderfully at home.

C. The Cost of Unity

It is a sad fact that most people want as much blessing as possible for as little cost as possible. But the kind of oneness that Jesus prayed for us to have is a oneness in the Spirit. That will cost us a great deal because true love cannot be expressed by mere words; it must be put into action. Jesus proved His love for us by paying the ultimate price. Now He calls us to lay down our lives for our friends.

What does this mean? It means that we must face up to our self-seeking and competitiveness and deal ruthlessly with them. It means that we must reach out to others, willingly sacrificing comfort, money, time, relaxation and ambition for them. It means that hobbies and homes will have to take second place to people. When we're living like this, our love for one another will be evidence of God's indwelling presence.

Complete the following:

No one has ever seen God; but ....

....

.... (1 John 4:12)

When we really love one another and live out the common life we demonstrate our unity and reveal to the world that the Father sent His Son to redeem it (see John 17:21). We hear so much hollow propaganda in our society. It's about time the riches of Christ were made known in action as well as word!

The apostle Paul was totally committed to the churches he served. He loved them and cared about what happened to them. Writing to the church at Philippi, he said, "Make my joy complete by being like-minded, having the same love, being one in spirit and purpose" (Phil 2:2). God intended the believers to be united in love. Paul longed to see this too. So must we. Our hearts must be open to teaching and admonition. We must pray fervently, and by God's grace we must do all we can to promote deeper love and unity among us.

Paul gives some very practical teaching on how we can do this. He says, "Do nothing out of selfish ambition or vain conceit, but in humility consider others better than yourselves" (Phil 2:3).

Selfish ambition is the attitude that considers our desires and goals as more important than anyone else's. It causes us to disregard the needs and aspirations of others and mars our service for God.

Vain conceit is basically pride. We think our ideas and our ways of doing things are superior to those of others. We end up thinking more of ourselves than we should and we despise other people and their abilities.

Selfish ambition and vain conceit are inevitable enemies of true fellowship (ie shared lives) and are hindrances to unity. Notice that when we have these attitudes in our hearts we are told to "do nothing"!

We must never be out for ourselves or think that we are better than everyone else. True humility considers others to be better and recognises their gifts and strengths.

Fill in the gaps:

Be .... to .... in ....

....(Rom 12:10)

Paul says, "Each of you should look not only to your own interests, but also to the interests of others" (Phil 2:4).

It is not wrong to seek your own interests. It is wrong to put them top of the agenda and care nothing for the interests of others.

What does Paul exhort us to do?
In Romans 15:2:

....

....

....

In 1 Corinthians 10:24:

....

....

....

How can you love others more? Write down some practical ideas and act on them. (eg Once a month I'll offer hospitality to visitors after our Sunday morning meeting)

....

....

....

This self-sacrifice reflects the attitude of Jesus (see Philippians 2:5-11). Your practical response to God's command to love others more deeply will be demanding and at times unglamourous. But God will reward you for your obedience and He will bless you.

D. For Better, for Worse
We can't look at the refining caused by relationships without reference to the relationship which, more than any other, requires radical adjustment in lifestyle: marriage!

Somebody once said that a husband is someone who stands by you through all the troubles you wouldn't have had if you had stayed single! As the women applaud, I will tell you men that there are two things that every man should know about women, and nobody knows either of them!

Marriage is hard work and sometimes it's very painful. When I got married I was totally unprepared to be a spiritual head to my wife. I was stubborn, selfish, unsupportive and, worst of all, unwilling to talk over any problems — which I interpreted as undeserved aggression towards me. I would react badly at any hint of personal failure.

Mercifully, God smashed my stubbornness by bringing discipline through suffering. Throughout these years of illness He has been working for our good. Our marriage is now better than it has ever been, and I treasure my outstanding wife more that anything in this world!

How should husbands love their wives?

.... (Eph 5:25)

Husbands, if you want a wife who fulfils your greatest desires, put this verse into practice and I guarantee that your marriage will blossom! Don't criticise or be harsh with your wife. Don't tell her that she must change. You're the one who has to change! As you work at your relationship, make sure that you deal with any problems daily. Don't let the sun go down on your anger. Pray about areas in your relationship which need adjustment. Pray for one another in your separate times with God. "Guard yourself in your spirit, and do not break faith" (Mal 2:16).

Fill in the gaps:

Husbands... be .... as you live with your wives, and

treat them with .... as the...

and as .... with you of the ....

.........., so that nothing will ....(1 Peter 3:7)

Wife, do encourage your husband — particularly if he is really wanting to change but is finding it hard. Pray fervently for him! My wife won the battle not by arguing with me but by praying for me. After she'd spent time with God she used to be so loving and gentle with me. I knew then than God would break my stubborn heart — which He did. She just stood back and watched. Actually it was painful for us both. But thanks to Him we have come a long way.

What, in a wife, is of great worth in God's sight?

....

.... (1 Peter 3:4)

Let's rid the church of male chauvinism and feminism! The world is looking for a marriage model that actually works. By being that model, we can reflect the greater love between Christ and the church.

Seek the kingdom of God first in everything that you do as a couple. Work at your marriage. If you have children, spend time with them, discipline them with love and pray for them. Be willing to make sacrifices. Don't become weary. Honour God in everything. Delight yourselves in Him and He will give you the desires of your heart.

If you would like to look further into the subject of marriage, may I suggest John Wilthew's book *Honouring Marriage* in the "How to..." series.

In conclusion
God wants to change us, to mould our characters into the likeness of His Son. Much of this work will be accomplished through refining relationships. We must resist the temptation to relate functionally and instead develop true friendships. We must resolve hurts and differences by putting Biblical principles into practice. Above all we must love one another fervently from the heart. Love binds everything together in perfect harmony and covers all wrongs. "Whoever lives in love lives in God, and God in him" (1 John 4:16).

---

[1] *New Frontiers Magazine* No. 1 1991

Chapter 9   ABSOLUTELY CERTAIN

Whenever the New Testament uses the word "hope" in regard to our salvation, it always means "certainty". In the world, suffering produces despair; with God, suffering produces certainty! We are able to rejoice in our difficulties because we know that:

suffering produces perseverance
perseverance produces character
character produces hope (Rom 5:3,4)

What doesn't hope do?

....(Rom 5:5)

This world is full of disappointment. People everywhere are disillusioned with life. By sharp contrast, the church should be full of hope. The Holy Spirit pours the love of God into our hearts so that we feel not rejected and despondent but loved and secure. God's unfailing love keeps our hearts free from disappointment both now and in the future (see Rom 8:35-39).

Paul says, "May the God of hope fill you with all joy and peace as you trust in Him, so that you may overflow with hope by the power of the Holy Spirit" (Rom 15:13). Our God is a "God of hope". When we encounter problems, He wants us to put our trust in Him and experience the joy and peace that He will give to us by His Spirit.

Although unbelievers can be joyful and peaceful in happy circumstances, they cannot be content when things are going wrong. Nothing gives strength and stability to their harassed hearts. We, on the other hand, can experience permanent joy and peace in Jesus.

A. An Anchor for the Soul

When the sea gets rough, the captain of a ship relies on the anchor to hold the boat steady. God has given us an anchor to keep us calm when the storms of life batter us.

Fill in the gaps:

We have this.................... as an anchor for the ...., ...

and....................... (Heb 6:19)

During a recent stay in hospital I discovered the reality and blessing of the hope that is in me. All around me were lovely people without the anchor in their lives. My heart went out to them. I shared Jesus with them and encouraged them to find security in Him.

Since it is impossible for God to lie, His promises are certain. Jesus has entered heaven, ahead of us and He is praying for us before the throne of grace (Heb 7:25). He is the great High Priest through whom we receive grace and help in times of need (Heb 4:14-16). Heaven is our certain destination — this hope keeps our hearts firm and secure.

Complete the following:

And..

.... (Rom 5:2b)

So we can be certain about God's love, our salvation, and heaven. As the old hymn declares:

We have an anchor that keeps the soul
Firm and secure as the billows roll.
Founded on the rock which cannot move,
Grounded firm and deep in the Saviour's love. [1]

112

B. Suffering and Glory

Peter has a lot to say about suffering. In his first letter he refers to the sufferings both of Christ and Christians. He reminds us that although we participate in Christ's sufferings now, we will share in His glory when He returns (1 Pet 1:11; 5:1). We can be joyful now. When Jesus is revealed, we can expect to be overjoyed (1 Pet 4:13).

What happens to you when you suffer for your faith?

....

....(1 Pet 4:14)

What will you receive when Jesus appears?

....

....(1 Pet 5:4)

We have a kingdom that cannot be shaken, a salvation which cannot be lost and "an inheritance that can never perish, spoil or fade — kept in heaven for (us)" (1 Peter 1:4). One day we will share in God's eternal glory and reign with Him for ever.

Read 1 Pet 5:10.
To what has God called you?

....

What must you expect to do?

....

What will God do for you?

....

God does not want us to be intimidated by Satan, knocked out by problems and pain or fearful of death. "He has given us new birth into a living hope" (1 Pet 1:3).

Correct this statement:
For to me, to live is Christ and to die is loss. (Phil 1:21)

What three things does Peter tell us to do? (1 Pet 1:13)

1..

2..

3..

....

The present is a time for action. God is looking for a people who will accomplish His purposes now while they "wait for the blessed hope — the glorious appearing of our great God and Saviour, Jesus Christ" (Titus 2:13).

In 1 Thessalonians 5:8 our "hope of salvation" is described as a "helmet". The helmet protects the soldier from mortal blows which would otherwise kill him or knock him senseless. Our helmet — the hope of salvation — guards our minds in the same way. It protects us from spiritual blows which threaten to damage our faith and confidence in God.

Why can your hope of glory be so strong?

....(Col 1:27b)

Paul said, "For to me, to live is Christ". Christianity is not essentially doctrine or ethics, it is a Person and a Life. The Bible defines eternal life in terms of a relationship with Jesus and His Father (see John 17:3). Nothing is more important than this.

C. Faith, Hope and Love
On several occasions in Scripture hope is linked with faith and love (see 1 Cor 13:13; Col 1:5; 1 Thess 5:8). Faith is being sure of what we hope for (see Heb 11:1), and our faith and hope are in God (1 Pet 1:21).

God wants us to excel in these qualities. Faith, hope and love will make all the difference to us as individuals and to our local church life and evangelism.

Jesus knows everything about every Christian, and He walks among the churches and knows the strengths and weaknesses of each one. He sees motives and actions, successes and failures.

In Revelation 2 and 3 Jesus addressed specific issues in specific churches. Read Revelation 2:2 and write down the first three things for which Jesus commended the Ephesian church.

1..

2..

3..

Now turn to 1 Thessalonians 1:3 and write down the three things that Paul commended in that model church.

1..

2..

3..

What three things are missing in the Ephesian church? (Rev 2:4,5)

1..

2..

3..

Both the Ephesian and Thessalonian churches were commended for their endurance, but in Thessalonica this endurance was inspired by hope. As we endure hardships and problems, we wait patiently for something which is unseen.

Fill in the gaps:

But .... that is .... is ....

Who .... for ....? But if

we .... what we..

we .... (Rom 8:24,25)

The Bible exhorts us, "Let us hold unswervingly to the hope we profess, for He who promised is faithful" (Heb 10:23). God will fulfil all His promises, so we must not throw away our confidence. Rather, we must cling to the Word and encourage ourselves by past experiences of His faithfulness to us.

D. Hope and Holiness

Our certainty of salvation and eternal glory with Jesus should affect our lives in a radical way. We should continually look for the Lord's return, enjoy a strong sense of eternal destiny and have an eternal perspective on everything that happens to us. Furthermore, our awareness and anticipation of the life to come should influence the way we live now.

Write out 1 John 3:3.

....

....

The apostle Peter says much the same thing. Having encouraged suffering Christians to set their hope fully on the grace which is to be revealed when Jesus returns, Peter tells them to — what?

....

(1 Pet 1:15)

Hope inspires both endurance and holiness. God wants you to rejoice in your sufferings, endure with patience and live a holy life. Allow the Spirit to bring revelation to your heart concerning these truths. Then let them affect your life. Resolve to live in the light of eternity and the Lord's return.

E. Hope and Boldness

Our faith rests on historical facts, not just on our experience. Jesus came as a man, He died and rose again. Unbelievers are without hope and without God in the world (Eph 2:12). They need to hear the good news and Jesus is relying on us to pass it on.

Read 1 Peter 3:15 and fill in the gaps:

Always .... to ....
to................................. who .... to give the
.... for the .... that.............................

How should we do this?

with .... and ...., keeping a clear
....

When it comes to witnessing, most of us do not feel very bold. How do we overcome? God's word tells us that "since we have such a hope, we are very bold" (2 Cor 3:12). When we fix our thoughts on glorious eternal things we begin to speak confidently about Jesus.

Write down a brief outline of the Gospel message.

....
....
....
....
....

If possible, discuss what you have written in a group setting. This will help you to be crystal clear in your understanding of the Gospel and it will give you greater confidence when you share it with others.

God wants you to be full of hope — free from any doubt or uncertainty about your future. His promises are totally reliable. If you lack assurance, meditate on the verses below and ask God to reveal the truth to you. There's nothing like knowing that your salvation is certain, that your destiny is secure and that God will complete the work that He has begun in you.

Romans 5:2b
Romans 8:35-39
2 Corinthians 3:12
Colossians 1:27
Hebrews 6:19
1 Peter 1:3

---

[1] Written by Priscilla J Owens (1829-99) and WJ Kirkpatrick (1838-1921)

Chapter 10   FINISHING THE COURSE

"I've started... so I'll finish." These well known words of Magnus Magnusson could have been spoken by God Himself! He has begun His work of grace in us and He will not leave the work unfinished. He never allows any of His promises to go unfulfilled. What He says He does. What He declares will comes to pass!

Fill in the gap:

...., that He who began a

good work in you will carry it on to completion until the day of Christ Jesus (Phil 1:6)

God started the work of salvation in your life. He will complete that work and bring you to glory. He called you because He had predestined you in love to belong to Him. He chose you before the world was made (Eph 1:4,5). You did not choose Him, He chose you and He has a fruitful and eternal purpose for your life (John 15:16). When God called you He justified you. He gave you faith as a gift and declared you righteous in Christ.

Paul traces the stages of our glorious salvation in Romans 8:30. Read it and add the six missing words.

And those he................................., he also ....;

those he ...., he also ....;

those he......................................, he also ....

We know how things began and we know how they will end. From start to finish, we have a living hope! If you are a Christian, God's

119

word promises you everlasting life. You cannot fail to reach your glorious inheritance. No matter how many failures, or difficulties, mistakes or problems there are in your life, you will finish the course and get to heaven. Nothing in all creation can separate you from Him and His wonderful love!

Such assurance of God's love banishes all fear of the future, of death, and of suffering. John tells us, "This is how we know what love is: Jesus laid down His life for us... There is no fear in love. But perfect love drives out fear, because fear has to do with punishment" (1 John 3:16; 4:18).

At the cross, Jesus was punished on our behalf. He didn't take 95% of God's wrath and reserve 5% for us to suffer! He took all our punishment and completed the work that He came to do.

A. A Job Well Done

"It is finished!" Jesus cried from the cross. He was not expressing relief. He was declaring a victory — and His words echo throughout eternity. Jesus is the author and finisher of our faith (Heb 12:2), the pioneer and perfector of His church. He died our death so that we might live His life. He was wounded so that we might be healed. All the wrath due to us fell on Him, and all the blessing due to Him fell on us. He took upon Himself our unrighteousness and clothed us in His righteousness.

Why did Jesus endure the cross and despise the shame associated with it?

....(Heb 12:2)

Jesus gave Himself for His bride, the church (Eph 5:25-27). He wanted to present her to Himself in splendour and holiness. He did not do half a job. He finished the course and after completing His work sat down at the right hand of God the Father (Heb 10:12-14).

We can expect to know not just the power of Jesus' resurrection but also the fellowship of His sufferings (Phil 3:10). His sufferings "flow over into our lives" (2 Cor 1:5). If we share in His sufferings we will also share in His glory (see Romans 8:17).

Paul says that "our present sufferings are not worth comparing with the glory that will be revealed in us" (Rom 8:18). If we suffer for Jesus' sake we are blessed. Let's fix our gaze on unseen things and look for the reward which will be given to us on that day when each man's work will be tested.

I would rather know Jesus and remain in a wheelchair all my life than be fully fit and go to a lost eternity. I want to build with the silver and gold of faith and obedience; of love and humility; of righteousness and holiness. I want to live the rest of my earthly life for God (1 Pet 4:2) and I am prepared to suffer according to His will and to trust in Him alone.

Read 1 Peter 4:19.
If you are suffering according to God's will, what should you do?.

....

....

Read Philippians 3:7-11.
What is God saying to you about your commitment to Him?

....

....

....

What is He asking you to do?

....

....

....

What's your next step (eg to memorise scripture)?

....

....

....

B. Ending Well

The doctrine of rewards is an important teaching which is sadly lacking in many churches. Moses, Jesus and Paul looked for their reward (Heb 11:26; 12:2; 2 Tim 4:8) and we are told that on the day when God judges each man's work we will be rewarded for what we have done (Matt 16:27; 1 Cor 3:14). It is therefore Biblical to look for reward. This knowledge should inspire us to live for the Lord and His kingdom. Our goal must always be the glory of God, but we must also look for the kind of reward that reflects our zeal for Jesus.

C.T. Studd said:

"Let us not rush out, let us not glide through the world and then slip out quietly without having blown the trumpet loud and long for our blessed Redeemer. At the very least, let us see to it that the devil holds a thanksgiving service in hell when he gets the news of our departure from the field of battle." [1]

God is looking for zealous Christians who will work for Him and pray in the harvest. He is calling us to live not for ourselves but for Him. While we're saying, "One of these days..." He will locate someone who is possibly less able but more available and use that person instead. We must stop procrastinating and start acting! When sufferings come we must refuse to lose heart and give up. We're about a great work and can't stop for anything.

Paul didn't let anything get in his way. Looking back over thirty years' of ministry, he declared with confidence, "I have fought the good fight, I have finished the race, I have kept the faith" (2 Tim 4:7).

Some years earlier he had longed to —what?

....

.... me. (Acts 20:24)

Is this your greatest desire now? God is looking for runners, fighters and perseverers. Would you put yourself among them? If you want to win the running prize you will need discipline. If you want to win the fight you will have to take bruising blows. If you want to keep the faith you will need endurance. God has entrusted you with the Gospel message. We must guard it and preach it — to the end.

C. Death and the Christian
When Paul wrote his second letter to Timothy he was expecting to die soon. Just as Joshua succeeded Moses and Elisha succeeded Elijah, so Timothy was to follow after Paul.

What two vivid figures of speech did he use to describe his death?

I am already being ....

the time.. (2 Tim 4:6)

There is a time for all of us to die. But for believers, eternal life is not just a future reality, it has already begun. The Bible tells us that Jesus has "destroyed death and has brought immortality to light through the gospel" (2 Tim 1:10). We have "crossed over from death to life" (John 5:24). God wants all Christians to have a healthy attitude to death. John Wesley's proudest boast was "our people die well!"

Let me give you some key points regarding the subject of death in relation to Christians.

a) Death has lost both its victory and its sting (1 Cor 15:55).
b) We have been delivered from the fear of death (Heb 2:15; 2 Cor 5:8).

c) Death is gain (Phil 1:21).

d) Christ's victory is so complete that death actually belongs to us (1 Cor 3:22).

e) Our death is precious to God (Psalm 116:15)

Jesus spoke to Martha about Christians and death.
From memory, fill in the gaps:

Jesus said to her, "I am................................ and ....

He who .... will...................., even though he

....................; and whoever ....and ....

will ...."

Now check your answer by referring to John 11:25,26.

On the occasion when I was very ill and thought I might die, I began to doubt that death was gain and became afraid of dying. I knew all the Scriptures and had often spoken boldly about death. Yet, faced with the very real prospect of going to be with the Lord, I was uncertain and fearful.

It is one thing to know the truth in your mind; it is another to have it firmly planted in your heart. I needed revelation from the Spirit regarding the truth about death and my inheritance as a child of God. I have now come through my fear and reluctance to die. I know that whether I live or die, I belong to the Lord. It is now my goal to please Him whether I am at home in the body or away from it.

Paul preferred death to life. He said, "I desire to depart and be with Christ, which is better by far" (Phil 1:23). God wants us to have this confidence too. If you are fearful or uncertain about death, let the Holy Spirit bring revelation to your heart. A correct view of dying will affect the way you live. You will not cling to your temporary body and worry about it. Rather, you will be excited about the new glorious body which awaits you in heaven (see 2 Cor 5:1-10).

D. Heaven

Many of us have a very vague understanding of heaven. Perhaps this is part of the reason why we don't relish the thought of dying. Heaven is a mystery; we're unsure what's waiting on the other side and can't imagine why death is thought of as gain. What does the Bible say?

1. Heaven is God's eternal home

Jesus taught us to pray, "Our Father in heaven". God made heaven (Heb 11:10) and rules over it (Ps 11:4). Heaven is full of God's glory and majesty (Acts 7:55; Heb 8:1). From heaven God speaks to us (Matt 3:17; Heb 12:25), answers us (2 Chron 7:14) and judges us (Rom 1:18).

2. Jesus came from and returned to heaven

Jesus said, "I have come down from heaven..." (John 6:38). The Jews could not understand how a carpenter's son could make such a statement. They knew Joseph and Mary so they naturally dismissed Jesus' claim to be God's Son (John 6:42).

After His resurrection Jesus was taken back into heaven. The disciples watched Him ascend and were told that one day He would return in the same way (see Acts 1:10,11). Jesus now lives in heaven. He is the King of heaven (Matt 25:40) and sits on a throne at the right hand of God the Father. Jesus is preparing a place for us in heaven (John 14:2) and He is continually praying for us. Everything in heaven and on earth is subject to Him.

3. What will heaven will be like?

Wonderful! It is reserved for those who are blessed by the Father (see Matt 25:34). He will give us new glorified bodies and there will be no pain or sickness, sorrow or sadness. God Himself will wipe away every tear from our eyes (Rev 7:17). We will receive our reward and enjoy the treasure that we have laid up for ourselves during our life on earth. Our knowledge and understanding will be complete, and all the mysteries and puzzles that have confounded us in this life will be resolved. Heaven will be a place of peace and rest (Luke 19:38; Heb 4:9). It will be far better than anything we have known or imagined on earth (Heb 11:16). But the most exciting part of all will be to see Jesus and the glory that surrounds Him (John 17:24).

4. What should our view of heaven be now?
Christians can rejoice that their names are written in heaven (Luke 10:20; Heb 12:23). We are citizens of heaven, our true home (Phil 3:20; Heb 13:14), the place where we really belong. Just as a citizen of another country longs to return to his native land, so we should crave for heaven.

While we are on earth we should live in the light of the glory that awaits us. Heaven will be everlasting. We will see thrilling sights and meet great heroes. Gabriel and Michael will be there, as will a glorious assembly of angels. We will never be bored or unfulfilled because God will give us responsibilities to enjoy. Those who knew us on earth will recognise us in heaven because we will retain our identity. It is an extraordinary and wonderful place (2 Cor 12:2,4). Paul couldn't wait to get there — neither can I! I'm particularly longing for that new body!

Most people think more about this present world than any future one. Their focus is on earning more, possessing more, looking more wonderful and doing more exciting things. But your home is in heaven. Your attitude to your heavenly destiny will affect your life on earth. If you know that you do not belong to this world, you will go against the worldly tide. You will fix your thoughts on things that are above and lay up treasure there.

So either you please yourself and live for this present age or you deny yourself and live for the future one. The choice is yours.

E. Press on... Win the Prize

As an athlete nears the end of a race, he draws on all the remaining resources in his body and makes one final effort to win the race. This last sprint often determines the outcome of the contest.

We have work to do for the King. It demands an all-out commitment to Jesus and to the spread of the gospel. We mustn't flag part-way through the race. We must run from town to town, country to country, continent to continent. Jesus is waiting for the Gospel to be preached to the whole world.

What will happen then?

.... (Matt 24:14)

God is restoring His church. He is stirring us to be zealous for His house and to have compassion for the lost. He is also helping us to see our sufferings in the light of eternity. Jesus watches as the bride makes herself ready for Him.

In these significant days God's people will be characterised by many glorious qualities. They will have exemplary lives, and a confidence in God which defies explanation. They will live in this world, but not adopt its values. They will endure hardship and rejoice in trials. They will not fear death but will long for Jesus' return. "Come Lord Jesus" they will cry — not out of desperation, but because they love Him and long to be with Him for ever.

One day the things that were made known to John by revelation will be made known to us in reality. He said...

I heard a loud voice from the throne saying, "Now the dwelling of God is with men, and He will live with them. They will be His people, and God Himself will be with them and be their God. He will wipe every tear from their eyes. There will be no more death or mourning or crying or pain, for the old order of things has passed away" (Rev 21:3-4).

Live for the glory of God and you will make a difference to the world. Remember that you and everything you have belong to the Lord, so don't treat your body or possessions as if you owned them. Rather, use them to honour God. Your zeal for the Lord will have great impact on believers and unbelievers alike.

Find your place in the church, give yourself fully to the will of God and seek to build up the lives of others. Then you will be a wonderful channel for the grace of God. His power will be made perfect in your weakness and you will be not a pain but a blessing to all you meet.

You will encourage other Christians by your faith and hope. You will inspire them by your patient endurance and your refusal to lose heart when prayers remain unanswered. You will provoke them when you rejoice in suffering. Your concern for eternal values and your longing for heaven will prevent them from being worldly-minded and unprepared for Jesus' return. And your contentment and peace will strengthen others who are going through painful trials.

Let's commit ourselves and everything we have to the Lord. Let's be holy and serve Him with all our hearts. Let's fix our eyes on eternal things and face life's problems with courage and faith.

---

[1] Norman Grubb, *A Cricketer and a Pioneer*, Lutterworth Press (1933). Used with permission.